MASTERING ELLIOTT WAVE PRINCIPLE

Since 1996, Bloomberg Press has published books for financial professionals on investing, economics, and policy affecting investors. Titles are written by leading practitioners and authorities, and have been translated into more than 20 languages.

The Bloomberg Financial Series provides both core reference knowledge and actionable information for financial professionals. The books are written by experts familiar with the work flows, challenges, and demands of investment professionals who trade the markets, manage money, and analyze investments in their capacity of growing and protecting wealth, hedging risk, and generating revenue.

For a list of available titles, please visit our Web site at www.wiley.com/go/bloombergpress.

Books by Constance Brown

Aerodynamic Trading (1996)

All About Technical Analysis (2002)

The Illustrated Guide to Technical Analysis Signals and Phrases (2004, e-book only)

Technical Analysis Demystified: A Self-Teaching Guide (2007)

Breakthroughs in Technical Analysis: New Thinking from the World's Top Minds (2007, Edited by David Keller)

Fibonacci Analysis (2008)

Technical Analysis for the Trading Professional 2nd Edition (2011)

Mastering Elliott Wave Principle: Elementary Concepts, Wave Patterns, and Practice Exercises (2012)

Advanced Elliott Wave Analysis: Complex Patterns, Intermarket Relationships, and Global Cash Flow Analysis (to come)

Books by Constance Brown

MASTERING ELLIOTT WAVE PRINCIPLE

Elementary Concepts, Wave Patterns, and
Practice Exercises

Constance Brown

BLOOMBERG PRESS
An Imprint of
WILEY

Published by John Wiley & Sons, Inc., Hoboken, New Jersey.
Published simultaneously in Canada.

Charts by Market Analyst 6, Copyright 1996–2011.

Charts created using TradeStation © TradeStation Technologies, Inc., 2001–2011. All rights reserved. No investment or trading advice, recommendation, or opinion is being given or intended.

Figure 5.7 © Robert R. Prechter, Jr.

For general information on our other products and services or for technical support, please contact our Customer Care Department within the United States at (800) 762-2974, outside the United States at (317) 572-3993 or fax (317) 572-4002.

Wiley also publishes its books in a variety of electronic formats. Some content that appears in print may not be available in electronic books. For more information about Wiley products, visit our web site at www.wiley.com.

Library of Congress Cataloging-in-Publication Data:

Brown, Constance M.
    Mastering elliott wave principle : elementary concepts, wave patterns, and practice exercises / Constance Brown.
        p. cm. — (Bloomberg financial series)
    Includes index.
    ISBN 978-0-470-92353-5 (cloth); 978-1-118-23515-7 (ebk); 978-1-118-22130-3 (ebk); 978-1-118-25977-1 (ebk)
        1. Elliott wave principle. 2. Speculation. 3. Stocks. I. Title.
HG6041.B748 2012
332.63'2042—dc23

                                                                                    2011046138

Printed in the United States of America
10 9 8 7 6 5 4 3 2 1

An ocean traveler
has even more vividly the impression
that the ocean is made of waves
than that it is made of water.

—Sir Arthur Stanley Eddington
in a lecture at the
University of Edinburgh, March 1927

Contents

Acknowledgments

I would like to express my sincere appreciation to the team at John Wiley & Sons: Kevin Commins, Meg Freeborn, and Stacey Fischkelta. The subject of the Elliott Wave Principle presents several unique challenges. The fractal nature of the method carries a message in charts that reflects on the bigger picture of the market in discussion. Therefore timing was an issue for the manuscript. I would also like to acknowledge and thank the efforts of the creative team.

There is no topic more difficult to edit as a number within a chart could mean a point to help focus the reader's attention, or it could be a critical number within a larger wave interpretation. The editorial team has helped us all by allowing me to use quote marks to define the start and end of wave notations. In practice this has helped my followers find it a little easier to read the unique dialog that develops within the analysis of wave patterns.

A special acknowledgment must be given to Robert Prechter, Jr., who saved this analysis method from obscurity. The work of R.N. Elliott might have been lost had it not been for his efforts. I once analyzed the S&P 500 market throughout the trading day before a real-time global audience for Elliott Wave International. It was the last step I needed to build my confidence that I could step out on my own and start my own company and Hedge Fund in 1996.

I cannot let it be unsaid that all eight of my books can be traced back to the confidence and guidance of Stephen Isaacs with Bloomberg Press. My loyalty to him explains the multiple publishers I have worked with over the years.

Introduction

After 20 years of experience helping other traders become more confident in how they apply the Elliott Wave Principle, I know how difficult it can be for many people. But over the years these people have helped me evolve my way of teaching this subject so that even the most challenged may finally see markets move in repeating fractal price patterns.

Why This Teaching Approach Is Different

We have failed to help you understand that price swings and Elliott Waves *are not the same thing*. Everyone begins with counting price swings since these are the easiest to understand, but the final result is disastrous. Why? You learn to ignore the internal construction of a price swing and overlook the rules that are intellectually understood, but then incorrectly applied. It is such a widespread problem that it merits the effort to try something new to explain these concepts.

Though our words are carefully chosen to match impeccable market charts, we have failed to really test your understanding by having you stop your reading at critical points to challenge your understanding. This is one subject that must offer ways for you to check your progress in small incremental steps before the learning curve becomes hopelessly entangled. Many traders on professional desks have told me they wish they had a way to test their understanding. Then they want to compare their errors with a detailed description of where they likely stepped off course. So often I see people correctly verbalize a rule or correctly identify and name an isolated pattern, only to then fail miserably five minutes later when asked to identify it in the context of a market chart. It is clear that my mission must include helping you bridge this gap. There will be numerous personal tests to ensure you are ready to move forward. I also have a method of drawing boxes to help you understand how connections develop within trends and corrections.

Another common problem people experience with the Elliott Wave Principle is developing a misunderstanding of what expectations they should be able to accomplish for their level of skill. There are in fact three major skill levels before the fourth level where you become truly proficient with a high level of expertise. There are several steps leading toward a level of proficiency. The steps in general are:

- Developing the ability to recognize the 14 price patterns as isolated components within larger price moves and to understand the basic rules. At this level you likely cannot apply the Elliott Wave Principle within a real-time chart and identify all the patterns connecting the whole.

- Developing the confidence to understand other people's wave interpretations. You should be starting to recognize when other people's charts contain major errors that warn you the credibility of the entire chart might be suspect. At this level you cannot develop your own wave interpretations from scratch, but you can recognize a five-wave pattern and isolate a few corrective patterns within the larger trend. You can also be easily confused, and an encounter with an X wave followed by a complex A-B-C in a daily report would be grounds for taking a break to grab a coffee. Your confidence level is on shaky ground.

- The next skill level is dangerous because this is when many people fail. You begin to correctly label static charts, but you cannot develop future patterns to describe how a market could move to your own price targets. You are probably proficient with the basic tenants of the Wave Principle, but you discover that applying these principles within a real-time environment is unnerving. This is a dangerous skill level because many people build error upon error and do not know they have misunderstandings. Their efforts start to fall apart like a house of cards as they think they know and understand, but the market proves they are missing pieces of the puzzle. They cannot figure out what they did wrong on their own.

- The next level is developing the ability to create future wave patterns that would explain and accompany the oscillator movement you expect to follow.

- Master: You have arrived at the highest level of proficiency. You know the Elliott Wave Principle is just a tool. It is now an intuitive working language to describe and develop a working game plan of how future market movements will unfold. You have no concern for the time horizon or whether you are given a market you have never seen before. The future swings track your hypothesis and show others that you are right more often than you are wrong. You know how to balance conflicting signals in wave patterns and indicators within different correlated markets and different time intervals. You can develop a wave pattern to connect these conflicts and explain how to bring the markets into sync with projected future pattern development. You have the ability to see the markets that are leading and lagging around the world *based on the internals of their individual wave structure.* You have the necessary proficiency with the Elliott Wave Principle to see how global markets can create a dominoes effect, and you easily lean on one market for timing while trading an entirely different market you know to be lagging. I should also add that when you are confused, you should realize that the rest of the world has been struggling for a much longer period of time. This is not to be confused by periods of mass public panic, which you calmly recognize to be a major point of reversal and opportunity.

You are now reading the first of two books on this subject. Here you will learn the basics and develop a correct eye for form, balance, and proportion of these patterns. The goal is to reach the last step toward mastering the Elliott Wave Principle. We all have to pass through the same steps of development to attain proficiency. Understanding that the journey ahead is a series of smaller steps will help. Releasing two books will allow me to add content regarding our global market top that is developing at this time. The cash flow analysis from the global financial patterns in 2011 is creating a second book. It will be of tremendous help for future study if I take the time to record these patterns and explain each for you. Therefore, know that you are not ending your journey as you conclude this beginner's level book.

The complex corrective patterns will be discussed in the second book. Only the basic patterns will be needed at this level. You therefore should not expect that with one reading you will be able to develop wave interpretations on your own or label all components of a trend. Both books will be needed to reach that level of proficiency. But even the beginner level alone is a powerful level of market position recognition, since many people do not understand market participant psychology. Few methods provide a sense of where a market is currently relative to a much bigger picture.

Having a realistic sense of expectations for your level of ability is also important to prevent becoming frustrated. Sadly, too many people complete the first steps and feel they have failed when they cannot perform at the highest level of excellence. Have patience and give yourself time. Try to set aside what you have heard and forget how difficult it may have been for you in the past. I will guide you toward each milestone to becoming a

Master. I've been taught by the best. My personal start was with Bob Prechter and Dave Allman, the two Masters who remain at levels higher than myself. But I know of no others when it comes to equity indexes and—my personal expertise—the S&P 500. My skills have been shaped and refined by the markets themselves and the traders that struggled before you. They have had lots of great ideas to help us all. Give them a chance to show you what worked and what made it easier. As an example, let me show you the missing piece of the puzzle that connected everything for "Mr. Lehman." The exercise you are about to do has since bridged the gap for many others whom I have taught.

Elliott Waves and Market Swings Are Not the Same

What is the first thing we do for you normally to begin explaining what the Elliott Wave Principle is about? We put a stick diagram in front of you with three long lines punctuated by two lines that serve to interrupt the trend. We assume that is the best place to start, but it is not.

In 2006 I had a very sharp individual fly in from Europe. He was responsible for all retail brokers throughout Europe for his firm. He said people had thought he was crazy, but he felt he needed to make a career change and had a sense of urgency. He wanted to be clearly on the side of measurable productivity as a trader. He felt he should have nothing to do with derivatives and wanted to focus on outright position trading. He was making a major career change and was willing to start as a junior trader. He had already been offered the job by another firm. What was the firm he was leaving? Lehman. He continues to enjoy a professional career as a trader today. The lesson from this story is to always listen to the inner voice we all privately know. He was out of the firm and had cashed out his options two years before the Lehman bankruptcy.

If it had not been for this individual, I likely would not have made the connection that we Elliott teachers fail right up front as we assume too much. He struggled and could not see waves in price charts to save his soul. Yet he could recite the rules and identify the isolated patterns without pause or error. I struggled to find a way to make the connection for him. Suddenly, in the middle of the night, a solution presented itself politely. He doesn't know how to read a price chart, to begin with, and I have never tested him to see how his eye works through the swing relationships within the price data. I then realized I had never seen anyone explain how to read price data with regards to balance and proportion.

FIGURE I.1 INTC, weekly

Source: TradeStation.

This will be a very interactive book, since that is the only way to really gain understanding with any depth. Your first exercise is to identify and connect the price swings. *This is not an Elliott exercise.* I have to be very distinct in my description of this task, yet vague enough so you have room to discover some important traits that evolve from the results.

Here is an important hint before you start this exercise. Consider the strength of a move and how you would trade it. Your task is to first study the weekly Intel chart in Figure I.1 to see by example how to connect one swing to the next.

■ ■ ■

Instructions: Make a copy, or plan to mark Figure I.1 lightly with a pencil in this chapter. You want to connect the swings *throughout the chart* by drawing a line from price low to price high and price high to price low. The first two swings are marked for you.

Turn to Figure I.1a and Figure I.1b in the Exercise Appendix at the back of the book when you have completed the task and compare your chart with

these. Do not read past the word STOP when an exercise is offered throughout the book, so you will have the opportunity to test yourself.
STOP

■   ■   ■

The results of your market swing interpretation will likely be a combination of Figures I.1a and Figure I.1b in the Exercise Appendix. I gave you the first two swings to set an example and numbered the swings that follow to add this discussion. The first question you faced was why I showed the ending of my first upswing on the second peak of a double top rather than the first peak. I personally view the end of the first up-trending swing as the first high of the double top. But I knew if I started the next major swing down from the first peak of the double top and ignored the fact that there was a double top, a few readers would be uncomfortable right from the get-go. I favor the first peak of the double top because that is where the trade ends. No other reason is needed. If you have a target into that high, you should not be waiting around for a retest into the second peak to see if you can make a new target that would be higher.

In Figure I.1a, you will find double bottoms in 2006 and 2009 near the pivots numbered 2 and 4. I marked the end of the down swing on the second low of the double bottom in each in Figure I.1b. If you feel you are at no risk until the second bottom into 2006 and 2009, that would also be correct. But recognize the task is to connect each swing, and you have to decide a double test into a major pivot to exit is better than getting out of a trade, reversing, and having to watch the market challenge the old high (or low).

Many people will not notice that my line drawn in the first decline did not acknowledge the bounce into the middle of the down swing. As a result, and this is very common, you likely gave no regard to the trend developing in any part of the swings. When there is a counter-trend move, it will have no impact to the longer trend if the retracement fails to overlap a prior counter-trend move. In Figure I.1a study the rising swing marked 1 after the two swings I gave you as examples. In the rally from 2004 into the high of 2005 there is an interruption in the trend when the market develops a pattern like an N. While the back-and-forth stall surely delays the timing toward the final swing high in 2005, the N pattern does no damage to the uptrend at this time.

There are two ways to test for what I call trend damage. The first is to observe whether the retracement overlaps another prior retracement of similar size or proportion. In other words, does the retracement overlap one that seems to be of equal significance in size and/or time duration? If there is overlap, the longer trend could be in trouble. Does the N formation within swing 1 overlap the range of the uptrend by more than 50 percent? No. Does it overlap the trend by more than 62 percent? No. Therefore this criterion recognizes the upswing in 1 is one complete unit and should not be drawn with smaller internal swings as building blocks within the longer swing.

The second test is a condition I take directly from W. D. Gann's work. Always be aware of the length of the strongest bar in the larger trend. When a retracement occurs, does a bar appear within the counter-trend that exceeds the length of the longest bar in the prior trend? Study the DJIA daily bar chart in Figure I.2. Within the decline off the 1929 high is a bar marked 1. It is a bar that is longer than any bar that developed within the preceding rally within this chart. If you study the bars in the box marked 2 in Figure I.2, the middle bar exceeds the length *of any strong bar within the entire 1920s rally*! The decline in the box marked 2 also breaks the last significant trend interruption that occurred in July and August of 1929. At bar 1 the pullback did not challenge this last correction within the uptrend and the only warning present was the length of the declining bar for a single day right near the highs. Never ignore that new benchmark. It is true in the opposite direction as well. It remains valid in today's markets that experience greater volatility.

When there is a counter-trend move it will have no impact to the longer trend if the retracement fails to overlap a prior secondary pivot. Let me repeat myself since this is very important. If the swings you have drawn begin to look like those in Figure I.1a in the Exercise Appendix, you are disregarding when a correction challenges a trend and you likely gave no thought to the slope of the corrective swing itself. Look at the swing from a pivot high marked 3 to a low marked 4 in Figure I.1a. None of the counter-trend interruptions drawn from point 3 to 4 break the downtrend. The smaller swings that interrupt the decline from point 1 to point 2 should not be drawn in this manner either. In fact, the small counter move up in the swing from point 1 to point 2 has a slope that is steeper than the slope drawn to connect the uptrend into point 1. The extra swings identified between points 5 and 6 are also unnecessary. If you have swings that switch from long swings to very short detailed swings within longer moves, you may be changing the time horizon of your trade as well. What I mean is you establish a position in one time horizon and then likely switch to a shorter time horizon when more detail presents itself. You are probably stressed to hold longer positions and scare yourself out of established positions easily. You do not know the time horizon you identify as your personal comfort zone. Therefore it keeps on changing within the chart.

FIGURE I.2   Dow Jones Industrial Average, daily

Source: Charts by Market Analyst 6, Copyright 1996–2012.

Now take a look at Figure I.1b. Notice the continuity of the swings and how the slope of each down swing is similar to every down swing. Now you can see each upswing has a very similar slope angle. The lines look nearly parallel to one another. The entire chart has a look of unity between the defined swings. It does not mean the internals have been ignored, but they have been determined to be components without challenge to the whole swing. As a result the length of a price swing is defined from start to end without interruption when it is not called for within the swing.

In the entire decline from the high at the top left of the chart to the price low we see five overlapping swings. *Notice the only real progress in the downtrend is in the first and last swings.* The swings in the middle chop back and forth across themselves, forming highs nearly in the same place. If you can see these relationships from top to bottom, you will be able to understand the Elliott Wave Principle and be right more times than you are wrong. Why? Because understanding the strength, angle, and speed of a price swing creates balance and proportion within the price move. These attributes are far more important than any wave structure label you could ever create mechanically. But when you cannot read the market swings for what they are trying to relay by themselves, you cannot develop Elliott Wave interpretations with any level of proficiency.

Are Attributes of Balance and Proportion Subjective? No.

There is one more area of discussion important for your preparation before we begin to tackle the Elliott Wave Principle itself (so named because the method was identified at first as R. N. Elliott's Wave Principle [of market movement]). It was shortened to just EWP, but really is just Elliott. Most of us refer to the man himself as though his name is synonymous with his method.

Examination of balance and proportion between the market price swings is extremely important before you ever begin to create an Elliott Wave interpretation through a chart. In Figure I.1b most of the down trend occurs in the first and last swings. The three middle swings change the timing of the larger trend more than contribute to the development of the price decline. I am always aware of these relationships within the price data.

To make matters worse, my best chart examples of "what's wrong with this Elliott interpretation?" come from professionals in the industry and from a software program on the market that clearly gives no regard to balance and proportion to wave structure within a price chart. So if you use a software program or the wrong professional as your guide, you are facing a tougher road. It is so much harder to unlearn something you have been applying incorrectly than to start with a blank page from which to learn. But either way, if you have to unlearn or start from scratch, I'll find a way to push you along the right track.

Balance and proportion are founded in mathematics. The skill develops from the study of geometry. Do you have to be a master of geometry to do well with Elliott? No. But understanding there is a mathematical basis to what we do will help you lift the veil of misunderstanding that this is all smoke and mirrors.

In the first exercise we started to introduce words like *slope* and *angle* into the discussion of things you should consider when looking though a price chart. Vectors have direction and movement and they are important considerations in technical analysis. Geometry shows us the relationships between points. I'm not going to spend time to look up the formula terms, since a few legitimate mathematicians cringe at my descriptions. But we only need to have a working understanding in order to apply geometry.

Look at Figure I.3, which is copied from a Russian book on geometrical constructions. You need only study the points along a line *OX*. The problem being solved is to construct the point *X*, inverse of a given point *C* with respect to the circle of inversion (*O*, *r*) I used to be able to whiz through problems like this, but long ago lost the skill and ability. But I retain the understanding that the solutions were serious works of art. I truly mean this. The page I have copied for you is just one of the steps toward a final solution.

Look at the spacing of the points along the line *OX*. Be aware of the spacing of the smaller subset proportions nearer point *O*, the area subdivisions between the circles, the flow of the arcs. Geometry develops a work of art. It is how churches in Europe and mosques in the Middle East are constructed. The symmetry and ratios between elements all have mathematical substance at their core. The Russian book is hardcore geometry

FIGURE I.3   **Balance, Rhythm, and Harmonic Proportion in Geometry**

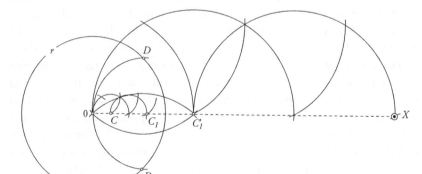

Source: A translation of the original volume *Geometricheskiye postroyeniya odnim tsirkulem* (Moscow: Fizmatgiz, 1959); A. N. Kostovskii, *Geometrical Constructions Using Compasses Only* (Oxford, UK: Pergamon Press, 1961), out of print.

problems and their solutions. I could not find such a book from an American printer. So how do you learn? Do yourself a great favor and purchase a book called *Nature's Harmonic Unity: A Treatise on its Relation to Proportional Form*, by Samuel Colman (Martino Publishing, 2004). It is a book written in 1912 with 302 illustrations that will blow your mind. If you want to develop a feel of why something is beautiful and why something else is not, get this book. When you "get" Elliott, your charts are works of art for the same reason. They will reflect the proportional relationships described by high-level geometric principles. Your job is to keep an open mind. My job is to teach you the principles and pace you through the steps that will take you to a level of proficiency that is pragmatic for your trading goals. Thank you for the opportunity; regardless of the experiences you have had in the past, you have taken the first step to a more successful future with the Wave Principle.

MASTERING ELLIOTT WAVE PRINCIPLE

CHAPTER 1

Using the Elliott Wave Principle to Evaluate Mass Psychology

In this first chapter I will help you develop a better understanding of balance and proportion throughout market price data. As the discussion evolves we will be able to consider the sentiment of market participants and why the price movement defines patterns we will find to be repeatable reactions in any time frame. It is so important to understand how to read price data and to see the geometric relationships that occur within a chart, that it would be very helpful for you to read this chapter and then turn to your own computer screen to use the tools described here to work with your own charts. Taking time now to make your own observations and develop your eye with regards to proportion will make the study of the Elliott Wave Principle so much easier for you later.

Geometry is the heart and soul of harmonious relationships in solids and flat two-dimensional shapes. Simply stated, the individual elements often have proportional ratios that connect one unit to another.

The study of ratios can become extremely complex. As an example, music theory is a specialized field of mathematical ratios with specific divisor properties. But we do not need to get complex right out of the starting gate because the math can be hidden behind illustrations of simple shapes and lines. Eventually you will want to answer why specific proportional ratios are more important in markets than other ratios. But the added depth does not necessarily make you a better analyst of market action.

Geometric Proportion in Market Data

Figure 1.1 helps me continue the discussion about balance and proportion that began in the Introduction. In my experience, the traders who struggle with the Elliott Wave Principle (EWP) do not see critical elements within price data. As example, one of the considerations about the health of a trend is to always be aware of the length of the longest bar in the time horizon of interest. Figure 1.1 is a monthly chart of General Electric. The longest bar in the uptrend is marked by an arrow and the number '1'. However, in a single month a decline developed from the high at '2' that exceeded the length of bar '1'. Some of you will not be able to see this, so use the boxes drawn to the left of the chart. The height of box '1a' is the price range during month '1'. The height of box '2a' is the price range during the declining month marked '2'. The width of the box means nothing, but if I dropped down to a daily chart, how would these two box widths compare? They would be equal provided both months had the same number of days. You will likely continue to study the bars and believe a different bar is longer than '1' as the final rally unfolds. But that is why I used a box as a ruler that is easily moved to new positions for comparison within the chart. The bar marked '1' is indeed the longest within the entire uptrend.

FIGURE 1.1   GE, monthly

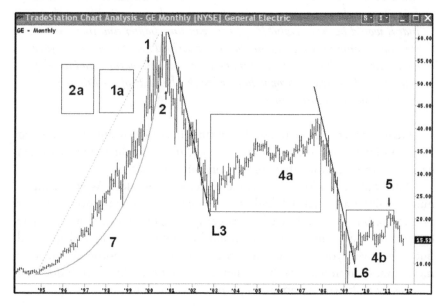

Source: Aerodynamic Investments Inc., © 1996–2012, www.aeroinvest.com; TradeStation.

The rally can be described as a parabolic move with a trend at '7' best drawn with an arc. Did you know a parallel channel of the same arc drawn as support can be set as resistance early in the move? It is never a parallel channel as parabolic rallies eventually go perpendicular. Nasdaq in 2000 and this stock both end the stellar rise before the two arcs have a chance to come together into the top. I'll let you try that on your own. As the GE chart is a monthly time frame, you should be able to copy arc '7'.

Consider the line 'L3'. It is drawn from a price high to the bottom of the price low for this declining swing. If I had drawn line 'L6' similarly, it too would connect a swing high to a swing bottom. The slope of 'L6' would have been clearly steeper because less time was required. It should be fairly obvious that the second swing accelerates into the bottom of the chart relative to the distance and time required to create the drop into 'L3'. But look what happens when I duplicate 'L3' and move the copied line over to the top of the counter-trend rally. The secondary pullback that follows the key reversal bottom actually uses this same angle to create a bottom at 'L6'. It is a strong entry signal although the rally that follows is weak. How do I know it is a weak rally that follows? It is a painful upward progression because bars frequently overlap prior bars in the advance. The congestion just above '4b' leads to a rally that is unsustainable as it is fully retraced. The pullbacks throughout the advance are deep relative to the range that ends at point 5. We do not even show volume, but the price action would be significantly less than the decline that tracks through line 'L6'.

Do you notice that box '4a' and box '4b' have a similar internal structure? The price data does not just move across the diagonal within each box. Both have a short interval when the upward progress is lost to an interim correction. While box '4a' covers more time than box '4b' to develop, the proportions within each box are similar. The interim correction develops about two-thirds into the time interval for each box.

Consider the pullbacks in each box to '4a' and '4b'. Study the space from the '4a' price lows to the top of the box. Then look at the correction lows at '4b' and the space to the top of its own box. Now consider these lows and the space under them to the bottom of each box. They are proportionally very similar. I didn't say exactly the same, but they have the same look and feel. These two swings are trying to mirror one another and that spells trouble for the price high at point '5'.

We have not done any Elliott Wave analysis so far, but your understanding of the internal geometric components is of greater value to you than the work from someone who applies the Elliott Wave analysis incorrectly.

Figure 1.2 is a daily chart of the December 2011 S&P 500 mini futures contract. There are three boxes. The first box on the left is followed by a rally that nearly retraces the entire move down that is contained within the first box. The middle box is clearly a significant market decline. Then a rally follows. The price bars in the area of 'B' show tremendous back-and-fill. Each bar is nearly retraced by the next. The lines connect through the label 'B' and the battle continues into point 'D'. This is a strong indication of market sentiment. The market decline in the middle box shows everyone is on the same side of the market. The people who thought the rally would break to new highs after the first box are caught. The people who sold early want more. The people with longer positions are in trouble when the low of

FIGURE 1.2 **S&P 500 Mini Futures, Daily**

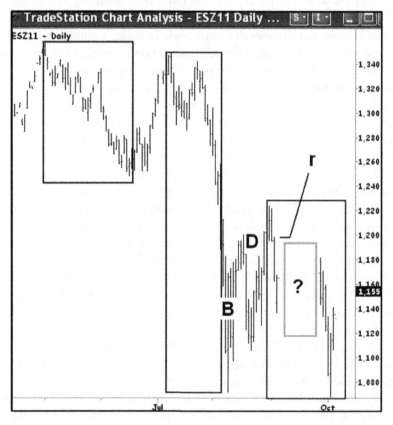

Source: Aerodynamic Investments Inc., © 1996–2012, Advanced Trading Seminar, www.aeroinvest.com; TradeStation.

the first box is exceeded within the middle. As a result everyone is selling. The key reversal bottom in the middle box would have very high volume. The price data that follows the middle box shows the battle between people believing the decline can resume to new lows versus those trying to bank profits. You also have some who think their fundamentals are aligned to buy. They have not learned you never buy a market that has just bottomed on high volume. So from the market low into point 'D' we see a fairly wild ride as both sides experience a choppy experience. This kind of price action is corrective. It means the final bottom is not in place. After point 'D' there is a drop that is fully retraced. A third box is drawn where the corrective move ends and a decline unfolds to the low just to the right of the middle box. The low should be inside the box, but you would not be able to see it as easily. It takes three swings to define the end of the correction that starts the top of the third box.

In the third box is a middle gray outlined box with a '?' mark. I removed the data. Do you think the missing data is a rally that exceeds the upper boundary of the third box? Could it be a rally that stays within the '?' box? How do you answer this question? Study the four bars that define the left side of the third box. Do these bars spend much time retracing the neigh-boring bar to the left? None. Is the slope of the decline for these four bars as steep as the slope in the decline within the middle box? Yes. That down force is back in control and the missing data in the '?' box never went higher than the upper boundary of the gray box. The two bars into the top of the third box form a key reversal. From that market high there are three strong bars before I erased the middle bars. You should know there is an old floor saying for identifying a frequent level of natural resistance. It is this: The market often retraces to the start of a third wave. In this scenario consider the bar with a line pointing to it as the point of reference. The 'r' stands for resis-tance and was in fact the actual start of the decline that falls back to create a double bottom.

What do you think the volume would be at the price low in the third box compared to the volume that accompanied the first price low under 'B'? It would be less. Oscillators would diverge to further help us define a bot-tom. We will add indicators after you have begun to study wave structure. But you do not need to see a volume indicator when you understand market psychology. The second decline will be the laggards, the inexperienced, and the weak hands tossing in their positions when they wrongly believed the first bottom was sustainable.

Study the bottom of the first box relative to the top of the third box. Notice the price high into the third box falls just shy of the bottom in the first box? Good. That relationship is something you must always be aware of as it will define one of our rules.

A spot currency chart is easy to read if you know how to decode it. Figure 1.3 is a daily USDCHF chart. There is no / between the currency references that reverses this order. But USDCHF refers to the U.S. dollar and Swiss franc currencies. To buy one you have to sell the other to pay for it. Therefore the first currency defines the trend. The first half of the chart shows the dollar weakening. Therefore in the first half of the chart the Swiss franc is getting stronger as the chart data declines. Then a major reversal takes place and the dollar strengthens as the Swiss franc becomes weaker. The Swiss franc was pegged to the Euro currency in an effort to weaken the Swiss franc. It is hard to sell cheese, chocolate, and such when your home currency creates a product value that is higher than at what most competitors

FIGURE 1.3 USDCHF, Daily

Source: TradeStation.

can sell theirs. Great for Hershey's, an American company selling their goodies overseas, but not for a Swiss-made product. So they made a change that caused this immediate move up in the dollar. Will it work and sustain this trend? Unlikely, because you will find government intervention often occurs right at the end of an Elliott Wave pattern. They get a strong reaction and then lose the battle. We will look at this wave count to see why this will fail when we have the skills in place to do so.

We can make a few important observations in Figure 1.3 without knowing Elliott Wave analysis. Notice the price action contained within a box. The price low at 'A' leads to another small rally and fails to reach the top of the small box. The market breaks and defines a small bounce into point 'B'. Here is what you need to really know; the closing prices into the pivot under 'B' never exceed the price low that defined point 'A'. If the market cannot close a bar into the range of the prior swing low, it has failed. Eli Tullis taught me this test and it has served me well over many years. He used to say "the market is no good" when this relationship between swings developed. It was an immediate sell because you knew you were wrong if the market could exceed the CLOSE within the price bar marked 'A'.

Notice after the hard decline into the low the retracement has the greatest reaction at the same area of resistance. It is marked with a double '??'. My question to you is to recall the exercise you did in the Introduction where you had to connect swings. Off the market low does the first swing up end at the pause marked by one '?', or would you consider the end of the first swing at the high marked by two '??'. The decline that follows retraces all the gains that followed the stall at the single '?'. Now we are starting to see the gray area that is the world of Elliott analysis. A price swing and a price wave are not the same animals. We don't need to answer this one right now. But the answer will come when we study the strongest bar in the rally that follows to the right.

Change your focus to the box above 'A'. Inside box 'A' is that pesky 'N' price action again that fits inside the rectangle. The first move up is a bounce that is counter to the larger downtrend. It is followed by a pretty choppy resumption of the former trend that leads to pivot 'A'. There is a short-lived upward move that chases many early shorts out of their positions. The rally does not exceed the first rebound. You just learned your first Elliott Wave pattern and it happens to be a corrective pattern. It is one of the easiest patterns to recognize. When you see the 'N' price pattern, put a box around it. That's how you can begin to study Elliott Wave patterns on your own. The price waves that create the 'N' are called a *flat*. It is always a *corrective pattern* that will interrupt the larger trend. In rallies, the 'N' pattern is inverted.

Notice the first swing down into a horizontal line on the far left of Figure 1.3. It has a price bottom near the top of the box that follows. None of the highs within the box exceed the price low of the first swing down. Now look to the right and find 'T'. There is a one-bar pause after the strong bar just to the left of 'T'. The rally resumes with a strong move from the same horizontal area as the top of the box. There is a lot of activity in this chart at that same horizontal level. Noticing horizontal levels of activity is something to keep in mind. It will help you later.

Staying with the same USDCHF currency market, turn to Figure 1.4 where a little more detail can be examined within the price data. This is a 360-minute chart and it has a few more price bars within a period of time than we would see in the daily chart. Currencies trade around the clock so there is always a question with spot Forex markets where to end the day. I solve the problem with a 360-minute chart. I have added my custom

FIGURE 1.4   USDCHF, 360-Minute

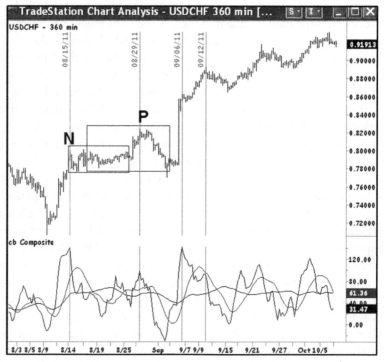

Source: Aerodynamic Investments Inc., © 1996–2012, Daily Market Report, www.aeroinvest.com; TradeStation.

oscillator called the Composite Index. It is an oscillator that warns when RSI is failing to detect a trend reversal. The formula and full description can be found in my book, *Technical Analysis for the Trading Professional*, Second Edition. A fast summary is the Composite Index has momentum imbedded within the RSI formula using a short period. A normalized oscillator that is forced to travel between zero and 100 is changed to allow it to swing freely. As a result, it can help answer questions like the one referenced a short time ago. Where would you end the first swing if you are on a mission to subdivide the rally that develops in Figure 1.4? Does the first swing end at point 'N' or does it end at point 'P'?

I would end the first swing at point 'P' because that is where the oscillator diverges. I also know moves never end where the Composite Index makes a new oscillator extreme. That said, the swing ends at point 'P', but the Elliott Wave count might end the first wave up at point 'N'. That is why you cannot assume price swings and wave structure are one and the same. Do not worry, since I have a game plan to handle this common topic of confusion.

We are going to spend a lot of time using oscillators as well to help build wave interpretations. But while you are on Figure 1.4, notice the oscillator high on 9/6/2011 is the same displacement as seen at point 'N' on 8/15/2011. Then the diverging pivot on 9/12/2011 is at the same displacement as the one that accompanied the price high at point 'P' when you compare the oscillator peaks on a horizontal axis. The oscillator is going to be of tremendous help to take away some of the guesswork that occurs when price data alone are used.

When I had a partner in Kuwait who was an options trader, his skills where entirely left-brained and he struggled to see geometry and wave structure applied to financial market data. Because of his difficulties I began to draw boxes since it solved language issues as well. He knew how many boxes were needed and I found it easy to draw boxes to represent future movement. It worked and we found common ground. (Left-brained is said to be our number crunching and fundamental side. The right brain is where we process 3-D images, geometry, art, whether a picture is hung straight, and so on.)

I began to use boxes to teach the Elliott Wave Principle and discovered that people loved the boxes! It made it so much easier for them. The more boxes I drew, the more I found we could apply the EWP to extrapolate a fast target using simple concepts. The best part is you do not need to know any Elliott patterns to begin to use this method.

You likely know already that trending markets move in patterns of five waves. If not, we will begin to look at this in Chapter 2. The third wave is most often the strongest part of a move because that is when everyone in the market clues in to what is happening at the same time. The people on the wrong side of the market have to cover, the people early want more, and the people left out on the side have to jump in. So everyone is one the same side. Knowing the strongest wave *is often the middle of the move* allows us to apply this knowledge in the following way.

Figure 1.5 returns to the daily chart for the USDCHF market. The chart contains two boxes. I have drawn the lower box from the price low to the pivot we called point 'P' in Figure 1.4. I then used the feature in TradeStation by using the right mouse button on the box to select 'New Parallel'. Any time you use this option it just duplicates the object. If you use different software, maybe you have the option to copy and paste. You get the idea—the second box must be an exact copy of the first. I then move the second box to the top of the first. I know, Fibonacci extensions would

FIGURE 1.5 USDCHF, Daily

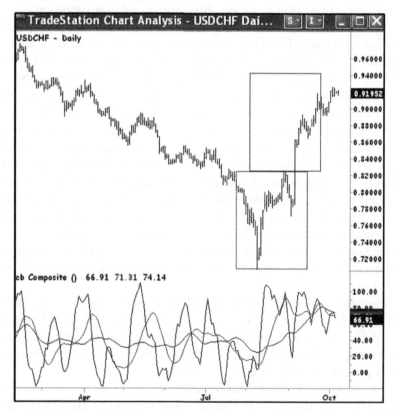

Source: Aerodynamic Investments Inc., © 1996–2012, www.aeroinvest.com; TradeStation.

tell you to move the second box to the low of the swing that follows 'P'. Forget it. We are doing something very different. Just put one box on top of the other. Why? The very strong bar that tracks inside both boxes is a third wave. It is the middle. Therefore I know it is half the move. The market is not quite to the top of the second box. That's good. The wave structure inside the second box is not complete. If you do not know it is incomplete, and you would not since we have not begun to discuss Elliott, we can use the market to confirm that we are making a logical projection this market will likely respect (see Figure 1.6).

Now we are going to pretend this market has already produced another move up that reaches the top of the second box. Subdivide the entire range created from the two boxes using a Fibonacci tool. The 50 percent subdivision should

FIGURE 1.6   USDCHF, Daily

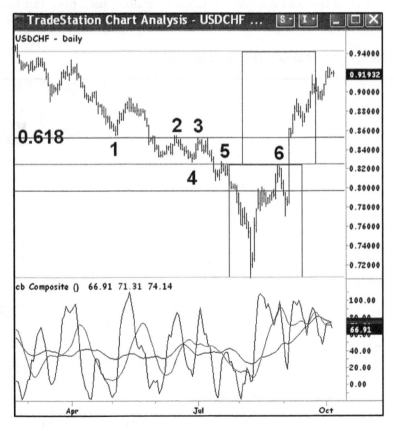

Source: Aerodynamic Investments Inc., © 1996–2012, www.aeroinvest.com; TradeStation.

fall on the boundary of the two boxes. What we are interested in asking is this: Did the market respect the 38.2 and 61.8 ratios as well? The answer is a resounding yes for the 61.8 retracement of the decline. This horizontal level was respected at points '1', '2', and '3'. Points '4', '5', and '6' respected the 50 percent area where I elected to define the height for the first box. I have to admit I saw the pivots at these levels before drawing the boxes. You will be able to do so as well with practice.

To show you this works for any market and any time horizon, a 22-minute intraday chart of the December 2011 S&P 500 mini futures contract is in Figure 1.7. The height of the first box is drawn. The range of the first box is subdivided into the Fibonacci ratios 38.2, 50.0, and 61.8.

A second box is created by duplicating the first box. To be more conservative this time, the second box is not added to the top of the first, but to the 38.2 subdivision within the first box. The market produces a pop to the right of the second box and respects the target by pulling back from this level. However, I know the Elliott Wave pattern into the top of the second

FIGURE 1.7 S&P 500 Mini Futures, 22-Minutes

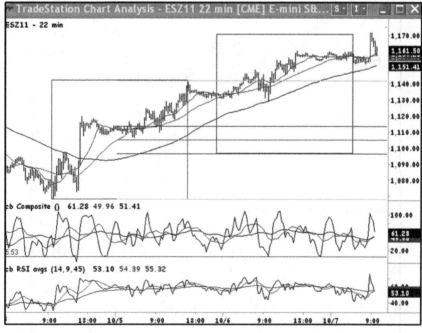

Source: Aerodynamic Investments Inc., © 1996–2012, Advanced Trading Seminar, www.aeroinvest.com; TradeStation.

box is incomplete. So now I have to use a longer time interval to create a new target.

Figure 1.8 is the same S&P 500 futures contract but displayed in an 88-minute time horizon. Okay, I need to get this one out of the way now as you will wonder about it throughout the book. Why do I use 22- and 88-minute charts? I like charts in pairs with time ratios of 1:4. I also want the new time chart without much effort. So why type a '2' and a '0' on the opposite side of the keyboard? Just type '22'. The '88' has more to it when you use Gann. What is important is using a software package that allows custom intraday time intervals. You need this if you position trade in long horizon or short.

Back to Figure 1.8. Now I am applying the use of the boxes in the S&P 500 chart the exact way described in Figure 1.6 in the USDCHF daily chart. It does not matter if it is three months or three minutes. The method does

FIGURE 1.8 S&P 500 Mini Futures, 88-Minutes

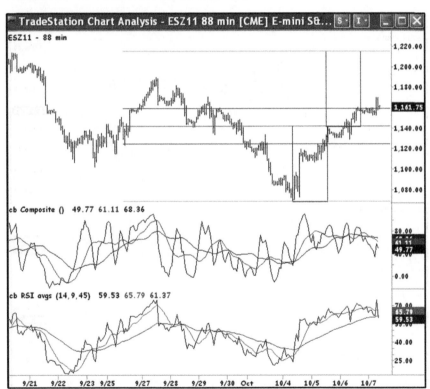

Source: Aerodynamic Investments Inc., © 1996–2012, Advanced Trading Seminar, www.aeroinvest.com; TradeStation.

not change. A box is drawn. It is duplicated and added to the top of the first box. Now subdivide the range of both boxes using a Fibonacci retracement tool. Does the market respect the subdivisions in past data swings? Yes. But there is one problem. The market has already exceeded the 0.618 retracement level in Figure 1.8. What to do for the next target as the top of the second box is a very long ways away? The answer is subdivide just the second higher box.

Figure 1.9 shows the subdivisions of the second box. The market has stopped at point '4'. Point '4' was the top of the range created within Figure 1.7. Now look to the left. Has the market respected the Fibonacci ratios defined by subdividing the second box? Yes. Points '1', '2', and '3' all track as pivot highs under these levels of resistance.

FIGURE 1.9 S&P 500 Mini Futures, 88-minutes

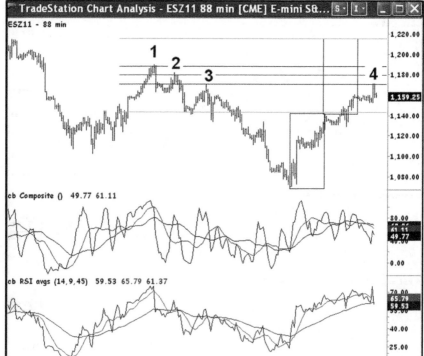

Source: Aerodynamic Investments Inc., © 1996–2012, Advanced Trading Seminar, www.aeroinvest.com; TradeStation.

Want to know how I did that? Want to be able to do it yourself? Then you will have to learn about the EWP. The Introduction and Chapter 1 have been primers to show you how markets move in proportional units related to one another. I was using Fibonacci ratios from different areas because you can add, subtract, multiply, or divide a Fibonacci ratio and get another Fibonacci ratio. I was showing you how this fact can be applied to your chart work. But how do you pick the right height of the first box? It is a secret, unless you learn wave structure and learn how to examine the internals that build the wave patterns. Waves are not the same as price swings. So there is more to it than most believe. I think I may have earned your attention to move on to the basics of the EWP. I'll continue the use of boxes so you also learn how to develop your skills regarding balance and proportional considerations within charts. Nothing feels better than getting into a zone where you are calling all the key price pivots for a period of time. These few charts are just the beginning.

CHAPTER 2

The Patterns That Describe Trending Market Movement

Now we begin to discuss the individual puzzle pieces that create the 14 Elliott Wave Principle patterns. Every market move can be described using just these puzzle pieces. You will be given a cheat sheet with the patterns in Chapter 4 to use as flash cards at your computer or to help with the study quizzes in this book.

People struggle with stick drawing representations of patterns. They seem to understand until they are given a bar chart. Then it all looks different to them and a blank stare appears on their face. I have seen this occur so often that I plan to try a different approach. Do not get hung up with memorization of the components like 5-3-5. That will come later. What I want you to learn is the feel of a specific pattern. That way you will recognize it more easily in different chart scenarios and when market character changes. If we look at patterns in many different ways, it is my goal to help you gain a better foundation so we can build upon these correct basics in the higher levels.

It is of paramount importance you truly understand that price swings and Elliott Waves are not the same thing. Everyone begins with counting price swings since these are the easiest to understand, but the final result is disastrous. Why? You learn to ignore the internal components of a price swing and overlook the rules.

Impulse Waves Create Market Trends

Impulse waves are strong trending price moves. Figure 2.1 is a weekly chart of a stock displaying a strong bullish trend. I have drawn three boxes. The boxes help to focus this discussion in several ways. The first wave up in the larger rally develops throughout the first box. *We label waves when they are finished at the end of the wave.* Not in the middle. Not somewhere near the

FIGURE 2.1   BBY, Weekly

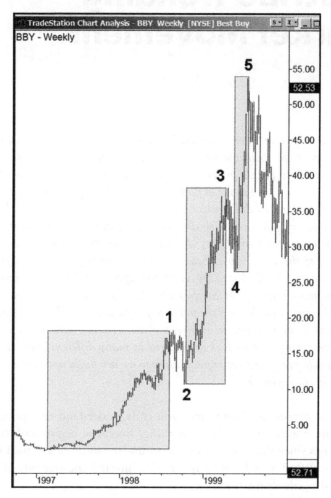

Source: Aerodynamic Investments Inc., © 1996–2012, Advanced Trading Seminar, www.aeroinvest.com; TradeStation.

side of the wave, but by being as precise as possible we label a wave just above the price high or under the price low that completes the wave. It is not always possible, but close enough will never do at any time with this analysis method. There is a lot to learn. Be patient with yourself. It takes time and practice. One of the problems for people is when they have to switch between different chart styles. Patterns easily identified in line charts do not transfer with the same confidence as working with bar charts. Therefore this chapter has lots of examples to get you on the right track.

Figure 2.1 shows the data at the top right corner of box 1 ends wave '1' up. Notice the shape of this box. It is close to square in shape. The internals within box 1 can be subdivided into a smaller unit of five waves. In fact, box 1 *must* subdivide in such a manner to create an impulse wave that will build the larger trend. As this is your first chart, we'll stay focused for the moment on the larger trend through the chart.

After box 1 is complete there is a correction that interrupts the forward and upward movement of the trend. The counter-trend move is not inside a box.

We then see the start of the next leg up from where the correction ends. The top of the box is marked wave '3'. The box is a rectangle that is narrow and tall. Wave '3' wasted little time to travel a distance greater than was gained within box '1'. The height and width of the boxes make for an easy comparison between waves '1' and '3'.

The internal building blocks within box '3' can also be subdivided into a subset of five smaller waves. Again, it is worth stating it *must* break down into five waves in order for the box to be a complete unit that can be identified as wave '3'.

From the top of wave '3' we see an immediate corrective decline. The bottom of the correction is marked wave '4'. A third impulse wave then begins creating the last box containing wave '5'. Once again, the internals in box '5' *must* subdivide into its own complete unit of five waves. The last box containing subdivisions of five waves is the toughest for a beginner. Wait until we have discussed a few more illustrations.

What you need to know from this chart is that the larger picture of a strong bullish trend is created from five waves. Waves '1', '3', and '5', or in this figure boxes '1', '3', and '5', are all examples of impulse waves. They build from each other and contribute to the larger trend. When interruptions occur to the trending market, there are two intervals of corrective waves. They move in the opposite direction of the larger trend. They also have a few rules to follow to allow them to stay within the same family of trending waves. Notice the bottom of the fourth wave. It starts the rally that defines wave '5' up. The end of the fourth wave is not allowed to decline so far down that it enters the range of the first box. When there is an overlap we immediately know something important about the trend that is forming. That will be discussed later in Figures 2.5 and 2.6.

It is impossible to discuss impulse waves alone without some mention of the structures that connect them. When one impulse wave ends, where does the correction go to that follows? Is there any consistency to where the

FIGURE 2.2   BBY, Weekly

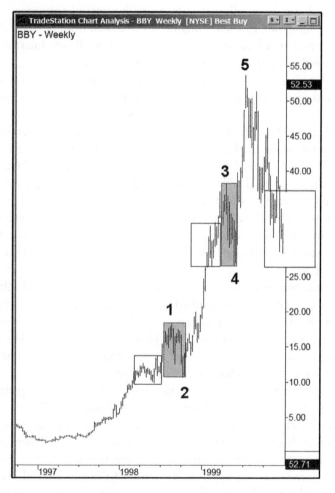

Source: Aerodynamic Investments Inc., © 1996–2012, Advanced Trading Seminar, www.aeroinvest.com; TradeStation.

counter-trend move will target? Yes, there is a general guideline you can consider because it happens so often.

There are now two gray boxes in Figure 2.2. This is the same chart data I used to highlight impulse waves '1', '3', and '5'. Now waves '2' and '4' are in small gray boxes. The labels for waves '2' and '4' are at the bottom of their boxes because we mark their endings only.

The price high marked the end of the completed picture of a five-wave rally. Notice the decline that followed. The very last swing down falls into a box that overlaps the *y*-axis on the right side. Look to the left and compare the shaded box that became wave '4' down to the clear box on the price axis on the right. The decline from the market high to the low has entered the far right box drawn to simulate the location of wave '4' on the left. When you complete five waves the correction often targets *the vicinity of the previous fourth wave (of one lesser degree)*. It just identifies a target range. Look to the left of wave '4'. There is a clear box within the developing move to its left that became wave '3' up. The clear box is the smaller fourth wave within the developing five-wave unit that defined the building blocks within wave '3'.

A similar reaction develops for the correction that becomes wave '2'. The gray box that contains wave '2' falls into the range boxed in within the first rally. The clear box contains a small fourth wave that helped to develop the unit we called wave '1'. Wave '2' found support and bottomed in the general range of a previous fourth wave.

Are there more accurate ways to identify the target? Yes. I favor Fibonacci analysis as one method. The steps I follow create target zones where multiple Fibonacci ratios cluster together. But I know the most likely target zone will fall within the range of a previous fourth wave when the larger trend is incomplete. Therefore understanding that markets track to the range of a previous fourth wave is added guidance for any price projection method you favor.

The last discussion put great weight on the internal composition of impulse waves. They must subdivide into their own five-wave patterns. In Figure 2.3 you will begin to see how smaller internal structures form. The chart is weekly data of a real market that will remain unidentified. It does not matter if the chart was a bar chart with semi-annual data or 60-minute data. However, the difference is how many more opportunities you have to examine the internals with greater detail. To drop down in time horizon is like rotating a new eyepiece and lens of higher magnification on a microscope. People who see someone change time horizons may not understand that you are not looking for something different to support your opinion that is subjective. When the waves are magnified and studied in a shorter

FIGURE 2.3 Subdividing Internal Wave Structure

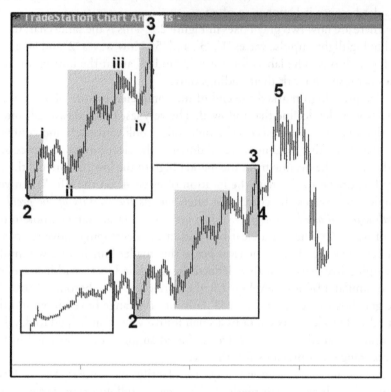

Source: Aerodynamic Investments Inc., © 1996–2012, Advanced Trading Seminar,
www.aeroinvest.com; TradeStation.

time interval it offers a way to examine the patterns to ensure they meet a
very stringent series of tests. Should an internal pattern fail any one of the
tests, the box method I used to show a completed five-wave structure could
not be drawn.

Figure 2.3 shows the first clear box contains wave '1'. Then follows a
correction called wave '2'. Wave '3' is a complete five-wave pattern that just
happened to form exceptionally clear and distinctive subdivisions. Within
the clear box containing wave '3' are three additional gray boxes. Each gray
box can itself be subdivided into a complete five-wave pattern that could
stand alone as an ideal example. The middle gray box ends a third wave
because there is a gray box on either side of it. But I could have taken the
middle gray box and subdivided it further for you. Wave '3' is copied above
the data to show you how the gray boxes would be labelled. There is no
question impulse waves have repeating fractal properties.

How to Label a Specific Price Pivot

The substructure within a larger pattern, like the gray boxes drawn within wave '3' of Figure 2.3, is the internal building blocks of the bigger picture. If the big picture has reserved the numbers 1, 2, 3, 4, and 5 to map the developing five-wave pattern, how do you name the other pivots without repeating the same numbers? As an example, the first box in Figure 2.3 was identified as wave '1' when it was completed. I cannot use '1' again without causing confusion. To keep all these building blocks identified correctly each subset will need a unique name.

We do not repeat the numbers 1, 2, 3, 4, and 5 again. For smaller internal waves use lower case roman numerals: i, ii, iii, iv, and v. But if I just referenced wave 'iii' when describing Figure 2.3, you would not know whether I was looking at a wave 'iii' within the first box, or wave 'iii' in the middle box that shows the completion of wave 3. So we write these smaller puzzle pieces in a way that you know what building block is forming and the unit it is contributing to within the bigger picture. It is like using a different line to identify the street, city, state, and country within a postal address.

QUIZ: Check your understanding up to this point on naming pivots within a developing wave. Put a mark at the price pivot where you think I am looking now.

Mark Figure 2.3 to show where wave $3'$ of iii of 3 has ended. The notation of $1'$, $2'$, $3'$, $4'$, and $5'$ has been reserved to label the five-wave internal structure of wave iii.

STOP

■ ■ ■

The solution is in Figure 2.3b in the Exercise Appendix.

Waves 1, 3, and 5 are impulse waves that build the rally from the end of wave 'ii' to the end at wave 'v of 3'. The middle gray box within wave 3 has already been identified as wave iii of 3. Therefore $1'$, $2'$, $3'$, $4'$, and $5'$ can be used to label the smaller pivots in the middle leg of wave 3. The top right corner of the middle gray box is the end of wave $5'$ of iii of 3. So the pivot called wave $3'$ of iii of 3 is located in the middle gray box.

The waves that create waves i, ii, iii, iv, and v are described as being one lower degree than the higher degree identifying waves 1, 2, 3, 4, 5. We can also state the smaller degree waves are subsets of the larger degree waves. Generally the word "lesser" is reserved for when you want to refer to the *previous fourth wave of one lesser degree.* We used this in the context of the discussion for Figure 2.2.

If you are drawing boxes in one chart, it is unlikely you will suddenly change to drawing massive or tiny boxes. We will look at a complete table traditionally used to label various degrees within a market. You only have three now, but that is sufficient until we arrive at Chapter 3. I think it is more important to continue our discussion about impulse waves.

Using Fewer Bars to Represent Complete Impulse Waves

You are learning several things by using boxes. The boxes force you to examine the internal structure and you have learned that every five-wave move can further subdivide waves 1, 3, and 5 into five smaller waves. When you look at waves in different time horizons they can display more or fewer bars because time expands and contracts. I have discovered most new to the Elliott Wave Principle will get this question wrong.

How many bars does it take to illustrate a five-wave move?

Figure 2.4 shows a 120-minute bar chart of the S&P 500. Not only are the three impulse waves contained within boxes (clear), but the corrective waves are in boxes as well (gray). You need to study the internals of these three impulse waves in the clear boxes. They all have five-wave internals. The first box is the easiest. The middle box for wave 3 will be difficult if you do not realize the bars above the gray dot create a small five-wave pattern to end wave 3. Wave 5 subdivided into its own smaller pattern of five-waves. If I went up to a longer time horizon the entire five-wave move might look like the right-hand insert that contains the same gray dot in Figure 2.4. Some of the bars compress into the new time horizon. It does not change the wave interpretation.

Now we need to be more formal with the rules.

1. Wave 3 cannot be the shortest. That means if wave 3 and wave 1 are the same length, wave 5 would have to be shorter than both. Wave 3 does not have to be the longest. Somehow people twist this rule. Just don't make wave 3 the shortest in comparison to waves 1 and 5.
2. Wave 4 cannot retrace into the range of wave 1. There is going to be an exception to this rule later, but it is a pattern we have not discussed yet.
3. The Wave Principle has a guideline demonstrated in Figure 2.4. Guidelines are observations that are often repeatable. They do not create hard and fast rules, however. When you look at the corrective waves in

FIGURE 2.4 Five-Wave Structures

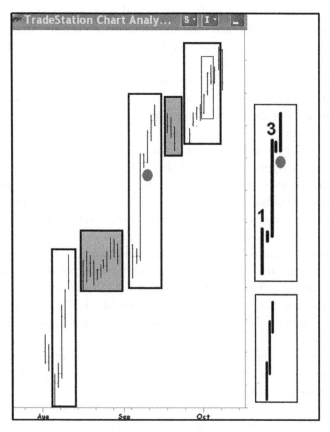

Source: Aerodynamic Investments Inc., © 1996–2012, Advanced Trading Seminar, www.aeroinvest.com; TradeStation.

gray box 2 and 4, one is about half the size of the other. This is the guideline of alternation. If the wave in the second position takes a long time to develop, the fourth wave will likely form in less time. If the second wave is complex in appearance, the fourth wave might just be very simple. The opposite applies when the second wave is simple and/or takes little time to develop. These alternating characteristics between corrective waves can be exceedingly helpful. Neither of the compressed insets in the right margin of Figure 2.4 illustrates the guideline of alternation.

Returning to Figure 2.4, look at the more detailed chart with five boxes. All rules remain valid. Now look at the upper insert on the right margin with a gray dot. Using only five bars I can easily represent a fully qualified five-wave swing. The gray dot ends wave 4 and it does not enter the range travelled by wave 1. The fifth wave in this bar chart is just a straight single line that moves up from the gray dot. We know our rules that impulse waves must subdivide into five waves so well that we no longer have to be shown all the subdivisions. We know they are impulse waves with five-wave internals because the fourth wave does not fall into the range travelled by the first wave and the third is not the shortest. So with five bars I know there is a five-wave structure present.

Now look at the bottom insert in the margin of Figure 2.4. If I took the bar chart in the upper insert and changed it from a weekly chart to a two-week chart, the lower insert is how the data would appear. With just three simple bars I can obtain a five-wave swing. The third wave is not the shortest. There are three impulsive waves. There are two corrective waves. Really, you may ask? Yes. The third bar retraces a portion of the first bar. Therefore, I know a second wave is present. The same can be said for the fourth wave being present because the third bar retraced a portion of the middle bar. I also know the fourth wave did not retrace the third to such an extent the range of the first bar was challenged. The middle bar is not the shortest. These three bars exhibit all the rules necessary to identify it as a complete five-wave structure.

Knowing that these three figures in Figure 2.4 all represent complete and legitimate five-wave patterns is critical in developing your skills to interpret wave patterns in any time horizon.

We have discussed only simple and extending five-wave patterns up to this point. Now we need to move forward to see how to determine if an extending five-wave pattern is complete or not. Extending impulse waves are much harder to work with than many think. It can be made much easier when you know where to start your wave interpretation.

Working with Impulse Waves in Strong Trends

Figure 2.5 is a market decline in the S&P 500. Many people have the misunderstanding that extending five-wave patterns are much easier to label than corrective waves. This is rarely the case. These moves that just keep going can be very tricky. Experience has shown there are a few unorthodox ways to handle these strong trends.

The first thing to do with them is to start your wave interpretation in the middle of the strongest segment. I can picture many expressions right now as

FIGURE 2.5 Extending Five-Wave Patterns

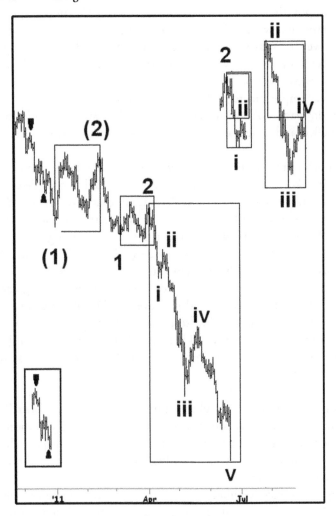

Source: Aerodynamic Investments Inc., © 1996–2012, Advanced Trading Seminar, www.aeroinvest.com; TradeStation.

I see the shock often. Our objective is to stay in sync and develop a sense of where we are within a bigger developing picture. Our livelihood depends on being right more often than wrong on the far right hand side of the chart. If we make errors in the top left of the chart it is not as serious. Begin looking at a chart to find the wave that is the strongest within the move. In Figure 2.5 wave 'iii of 3' is the strongest. I am referencing the entire length of the decline from the end of wave 'ii' up to the end of wave 'iii' down. My first label was to put 'iii' on the pivot low of this move. We know impulse waves must contain five waves. Wave 'iii' completes five-waves from the pivot marked wave 'ii'. Wave 'ii' is a correction. Next, find its counterpart correction. The bounce off of wave 'iii' is very clean and direct with an ending we know is wave 'iv' up.

It is very important to make this next consideration.

How do waves 'ii' and waves 'iv' compare in size? Consider both distance travelled and time required to develop the correction.

1. They both retrace to previous fourth waves of one lesser degree.
2. Wave 'ii' takes about half the time that was needed to complete wave 'iv'.
3. Wave 'ii' travels about a third of the way up that wave 'iv' travelled. But the distances travelled by waves 'ii' and 'iv' are proportionally about the same relative to the trending segment they are correcting.
4. Consider where waves 'ii' and 'iv' divide waves 'i' and wave 'iii'. The top right insert in Figure 2.5 will help you.
5. Then consciously consider any space over 'ii' until an imaginary horizontal level that marks the end of wave '2'. Do likewise for the space from '2' until an imaginary horizontal level marking the end of wave '(2)'. You simply consider the vertical height and do not give any consideration to the slope of the decline. Now you should be able to sense they are somewhat similar.

All of the patterns and substructures of the Elliott Wave Principle require these ratio comparisons between internal units. If you didn't know geometry beforehand, you are learning it now. The areas of space above and below the midlines are not far off when comparing one to the other. It doesn't have to be exact.

In my experience, engineers by training have the greatest trouble with this. As odd as it may sound, if you are having a hard time with this comparison it is time to take remedial action! Sign up for an art class. Not just any class. Start with still life. As you draw a Venetian or Greek vase you suddenly have to take notice of what is called positive and negative space. The positive space is the silhouette form of the vase itself. The negative space is the void of space behind the object. Our bars of data are the positive space. The blank space inside a box behind the data is the negative space. Learn to use it.

We will not look at the shapes and proportional guidelines between corrective waves until the next chapter. But we could not escape a brief introduction to complete Figure 2.5.

From the price high marked wave 'iv' there is a five-wave decline. So immediately label the price low as wave 'v'. I know we don't have wave 'i' identified. It is going to be harder and does not change the message of the price low marked wave 'v'.

QUIZ: Where does a market go after a five-wave decline? Using Figure 2.5, draw a box around the target range where a corrective bounce would likely target from the low marked wave 'v of 3'. The answer is in the Exercise Appendix in Figure 2.5b.

STOP

■ ■ ■

This is much harder than it first looks. It will test many parts of your understanding to this point. If you drew a line to any spot within the gray box in Figure 2.5b you got it! However, you may not entirely know how you got it right.

You must first recognize that wave 'v' ends a five-wave pattern that began from wave '2'. Therefore, the fourth wave we must use, which is of one lesser degree, is wave 'iv'. Why? Because we are projecting the target for wave '4' up within the developing wave '(3)' decline. I have not given you the complete table of all the ways to mark higher and lower degrees. That comes in Chapter 4, but the pattern is clear about what a number in parentheses means. See the coils at the top? I have three different degrees in the works. We have wave '(1)', wave '1', and wave 'i'. They all need to satisfy five-wave patterns for their own specified degree.

You extend the range travelled by wave 'iv' to the right to create the range we call the previous fourth wave of one lesser degree. The small fourth wave in a gray circle with an 'x' through the data is incorrect. You identified a fourth wave, but it is only a small fourth wave that helped to build wave 'v'.

New Quiz.

QUIZ: Using Figure 2.5b in the Appendix, consider wave '4' to be at the top of the line drawn from wave 'v'.

1. How many waves will develop between the top of wave '4' and the completion of wave '5'?
2. Wave '5' falls below the price low marked wave 'v'. What wave of larger degree does it end?
3. Wave (4) will then target what area in Figure 2.5b?

STOP

■ ■ ■

The answers to the questions are:

1. Wave '5' must develop a five-wave pattern because it is an impulse wave within an extending larger impulse wave.
2. Wave (3). We therefore would name it wave '5 of (3)' to be more precise.
3. The same gray box. You would have to see the actual correction of wave '4' to know the full range that defined the pattern of wave '4'. But you know the line drawn into the range of wave 'iv' has to be within wave '4'. Therefore you are seeing why fourth waves of different degrees tend to retarget similar areas in a chart. This can be very helpful when it is hard to see the internal subdivisions. Two back-to-back corrections can often be marked 'iv' and '4' and then work backwards. Samples will come later in the next chapter. You do not need to know corrective patterns to understand where a target area will reside in the data.

Before we move away from Figure 2.5, there is a small insert on the bottom left. The bullets mark the top and bottom of a third wave within the wave (1) from the top of the screen so you can see the subdivision more clearly. The higher boxes drawn for waves (2) and wave '2' enclose the exact same pattern. Remember the 'N'? They are back. These patterns are corrective *flats* and the lower overlaps the higher one. The lower one is smaller than the first one. When you see a market creating mirror duplicates and getting smaller, the market is coiling for one heck of a big move.

Because we started in the middle with the strongest segment, we know how many waves are missing in the larger picture. But what if we bounce into the range of wave 'iv' and the market has a complete meltdown that is even longer than wave '3'? You likely have a new midline for the move. Just go with it. You were not wrong, as the work and wave interpretations you made kept you on the right side of the market. That is the whole point. We are trading market moves and not being paid for gorgeous charts and beautiful labels.

The method of using boxes is valuable because it makes it very clear how a market is developing internal building blocks. I'd like to spend more time on this in Figure 2.6.

Figure 2.6 is the weekly Kuwait Stock Market Index. This is the first time you have worked with a line on close chart style. Wave structure is no different using a line than what you have seen in the prior charts. In fact, it sometimes makes it easier to see the pattern developing.

FIGURE 2.6 Kuwait Stock Index, Weekly

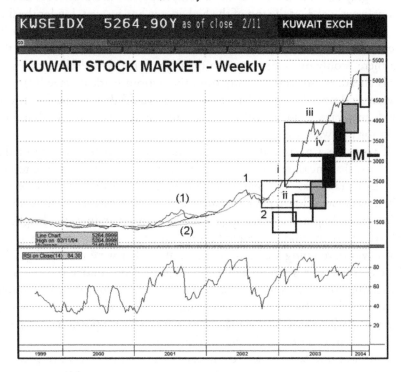

Where do we start? At the middle, and we need to select the strongest leg up within the rally. The strongest wave is located and a horizontal line is drawn in the approximate middle. The mid-line is marked with an 'M' to the right. Above and below the line you will find two black boxes. They mark the start and end of that wave. We know the top of the box will be wave 'iii'. The bottom of the clear box ends wave 'ii'. We know the middle and the faint turns within the range clearly define a five-wave structure. The second and fourth waves are nothing more than a slight pause, but that is all that is needed.

Two gray boxes are drawn, one below the black boxes and one above the higher black box. The lower area is extended to the left so you can see it tracks from the low of wave '2' to the end of wave 'i'. Wave 'iii' has an enclosed box. The correction marking wave 'iv' down falls back inside the middle box. The swing that follows defines the higher gray box. Could the two gray boxes and black create a complete five-wave unit? Yes. But do not put wave 'v of 3' at the top of the higher gray box just yet. Under the first gray box there are two clear boxes showing first wave swings that must be offset with fifth waves into the top to end the move. But when we look at the high there is only one clear box into the high. It means a decline and final rally is ahead. It will end the rally from the bottom marked wave '(2)' and therefore end wave '3' up. A larger correction would then begin, but it will only define wave 4 down. All the boxes in Figure 2.6 show the building blocks for just wave (3).

If you take a measured move from the midline to the bottom of the lower box, that measured move added to the midline will end at the top of the higher gray box. The market is moving in a mirror image above the midline as below. This market displays a strong trend, but at this time it was neither expanding nor contracting. If it had been expanding, the height of the boxes above the midline would be longer than those below the line. If the market was developing waves over the midline that were contracting, the height of these boxes would not be as high as those under the midline. Contracting box heights warn a market is weakening. Elongating boxes over the midline show the market is becoming parabolic. The use of boxes will force you to be aware of balance, symmetry, and proportion—all good things to keep us on the right side of the market.

You have one last chance to understand extending five-wave patterns before I toss you out of the nest to take a test, so study Figure 2.7 very closely.

Figure 2.7 gives you waves (1), (2), (3), and (4). The common error made by many people is to jump down to the bottom of the swing and write (5) under the lowest price pivot. Wrong. How many waves must there be in wave (5)? It must define 5 swings where the fourth wave does not retrace into the first wave and wave three doesn't become the shortest. There is only one swing that meets all these rules. Wave (5) ends at the third pivot low from the bottom of the chart. To the right is the same data. However, I have pulled the bars apart that define the waves. The last pattern into the bottom contains a three-wave swing down to a low marked 'B'. It is a middle leg of a corrective pattern you will study in the next chapter.

In this example wave (5) becomes a pivot many find very confusing. It is referred to as the *orthodox* low (or high in a bull trend). It is the pivot that completes the five-wave decline. However, the market tries to keep on going. Do not try to stuff those extra swings into your impulse wave. The data that forms below wave 'A' begins to overlap. There is a serious middle leg that overlaps the first swing down from 'A'. The entire move down from 'A' to the low cannot remain true to the rules of a developing five-wave pattern.

FIGURE 2.7 Extending Five-Wave Patterns

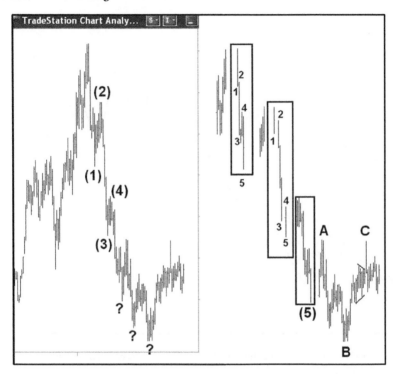

Source: Aerodynamic Investments Inc., © 1996–2012, Advanced Trading Seminar, www.aeroinvest.com; TradeStation.

Something else is going on. It is a leg within a corrective pattern. Oscillators will diverge and the volume will be lower than the volume into the final bar that offered capitulation at the end of wave (5). This chart is the most important chart I can offer you to prove price swings and Elliot Waves are not the same thing.

Let's see if you have it etched in stone before moving on.

QUIZ: This is your first serious challenge. But you will be given several hints to lead to your success.

Scan or make a copy of Figure 2.8. Use the numbers (1), (2), (3), (4), and (5) for higher degrees and numbers 1, 2, 3, 4, and 5 for lower degrees. You will not be trying to label the internals of waves (2) or (4). Just mark where waves (2) and (4) must end at the appropriate time.

Begin by putting a dot near the middle of the strongest swing within the entire rally.

FIGURE 2.8   Extending Five-Wave Pattern Exam

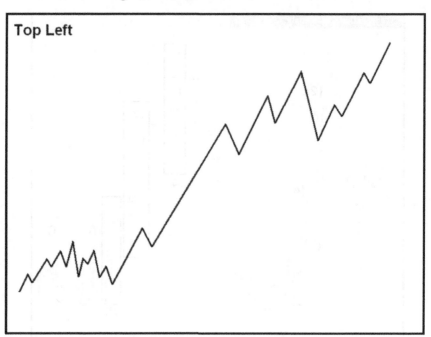

Top Left

Source: Aerodynamic Investments Inc., © 1996–2012, Advanced Trading Seminar,
www.aeroinvest.com.

Mark the end of wave 5 of (3).

Take the time now to label the internal swings within wave (3).

Even though you do not know corrective patterns, you can make no
mistakes provided you continually remind yourself that *impulse waves must
contain five waves.*

Draw a box to show the complete unit we call wave (3). Are there five
waves inside the box? NO? Fix it! You will have to start over.

We know wave (2) leads into wave (3), so you know where the end of
wave (2) is located. Mark it.

Then find five waves that satisfy the rules for wave (1) and wave (5). It
will be easier to work on wave (5) first in this chart. Put waves (1) and (5)
inside their own box. You will be left with swings you cannot name. Just
leave them outside the boxes.

Compare your answer to the one in the Exercise Appendix in Figure 2.8b.
STOP

■ ■ ■

How did you do? If you got it, fantastic! But there are several common places people fall into trouble. The biggest problem is ignoring the rules for an impulse wave. Every impulse wave must have internals with five waves. Looking at Figure 2.8b there is a peak that is higher than the end of wave (3). That is the one that causes much of the trouble. There is no possible way to create five internal waves when you label the swing and ignore the internal wave structure. You likely put your dot on the right bar and then ignored the rest. Normally the only mistake in wave (5) is getting the internal waves marked incorrectly. You cannot use the lower case roman numerals because you were given the larger degree as a number in parentheses. If you can see five-waves within wave (5), wave (4) was easy to label as it ends the exact pivot that begins wave (5). It does not matter that the middle leg within wave (4) tries to make a new high above the end of wave (3). This happens all the time. It will be discussed more in the next chapter.

All the swings that form within wave (2) mess with people's minds. Do not let them! From the far left side of the chart you can easily find five-waves. End of story. You know that is the end of wave (1). You already have wave (2) marked as it began wave (3). What to call wave (2) and how to identify all the waves within wave (2) is not the problem for you at this time. You have found a way to bridge your own skill level. That is what is needed for the moment. I will ask you to label the internal swings of waves (2) and (4) another time when we cover corrective wave patterns in Chapter 3.

When you begin to learn Elliott Wave patterns, the box idea will move you faster through the learning curve.

Termination Diagonal Triangles: An Introduction

The Termination Diagonal Triangle is a pattern that terminates trends and is the most common wedge. It is found in fifth-wave positions most often so they are viewed as impulse waves. But you will learn later that they can end corrective patterns as well. They complete a larger trend, and to really understand the internals of these patterns you need to study the basic corrective waves that follow in Chapter 3. So we will only take a quick look at the basic structure now and the message the pattern will carry. Then after we discuss corrections, I will be able to offer you a far more meaningful discussion in Chapter 4 when we have the tools needed to develop a deeper understanding.

The Termination Diagonal Triangle has a distant rare cousin. The internal structure of the second type has a very different way of developing.

FIGURE 2.9 Termination Diagonal Triangle

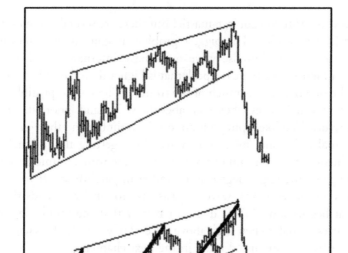

Source: Aerodynamic Investments Inc., © 1996–2012, Advanced Trading Seminar,
www.aeroinvest.com; TradeStation.

The common diagonal pattern carries a message that the trend is exhausted
and the other leads to new trends. There will be no confusion about which
one is forming, but you need not worry about the second type until we
revisit it. Focus now on the most common Diagonal Triangle pattern. It
often develops in a fifth wave position to end a trend. It is illustrated by
the S&P 500 during an intraday move in Figure 2.9. All Diagonal Triangle
patterns have a wedge-shaped appearance to them. There will be three
overlapping waves creating higher lows and higher highs in bull market
trends. In bear markets the tops are progressively lower and the bottoms
make new lows for each swing. The outer trend lines appear to wedge and
converge gradually towards one another.

The slope of waves 1, 3, and 5 will become more flat in each impulse
wave position. This is illustrated in Figure 2.9. Most people step into these

FIGURE 2.10 S&P 500 Mini Futures

Source: Aerodynamic Investments Inc., © 1996–2012, Advanced Trading Seminar, www.aeroinvest.com; TradeStation.

patterns too early, thinking they are complete when they are not. We are anxious to see them end because the message they carry is that a sharp trend reversal is coming that will retrace the entire length of the pattern back to its origin. They are money-makers when they are read correctly. But they are not as simple as they may first appear to be.

For now it will suffice to know this wedge looking pattern is a trend killer and considered to be a valid impulse wave that develops in the fifth wave position of developing trends. We will look at them in more detail in Chapter 4.

If you struggled with the test in Figure 2.8, here is a new test to help you examine your understanding of extending impulse waves.

QUIZ: Use Figure 2.10 to create a complete five wave decline from top to bottom. You will be adding swings to complete the impulse wave.

This time it is not a stick diagram. When you have your wave interpretation completed, check the Exercise Appendix in Figure 2.10b. Don't move ahead until you see it. Here is a hint for you to consider.

The Fibonacci retracement targets are resistance levels and were never intended to be support target levels that the market has fallen through. The entire move down is incomplete. Can you draw boxes that would suggest where the missing waves could develop?

CHAPTER 3

The Basic Patterns That Describe Corrective Market Movement

Impulse waves were examined in the last chapter. Now we need to examine the corrective waves that move counter-trend and connect the impulse waves together. This chapter will give you basic patterns we will use to identify simple corrections and, in the second book, we will examine how the same basic patterns develop more complex and time consuming structures. The more advanced work will always use the same basic patterns we are about to discuss.

Corrective patterns get a bad rap because the more complex ones can be described in different ways. But the number of puzzle pieces you have to work with is a very small list. Therefore, if different corrective patterns were shades of color, a blue puzzle piece will always be blue. A green one must always be green and fully satisfy the criteria that define "green." If you can use two green puzzle pieces and one blue one to describe a complete correction, that would be fine. If you favor using two blue patterns and one green, that too is fine provided the criteria that define each color have not been violated. Both scenarios must not violate the pattern rules and both will end at the exact same price pivot. Therefore, they would both carry the same message about the future market movement that would follow.

These corrective patterns are very well defined. The problem resides in the fact that people start making it up. You can have your own method of creating wave structure—Nelly Waves, Harmonic Waves, even George Lane Waves—but do not call these practices part of the Elliott Wave Principle

(EWP) when the underlying tenants of the EWP are not strictly followed. It doesn't mean other approaches to wave analysis are incorrect. But do not lead people to think a method is the Wave Principle when in fact something entirely different is being applied. You will soon discover it is not as difficult as you may have first experienced or heard. But do not judge a method until it is correctly applied.

How to Examine Corrective Price Movement

Begin with the problem people have of matching line diagrams with actual market data right now. I do not want you to be concerned with any prior training you may have had up to this point. Tables of 3-3-5 and such need to go off the desk and out of sight. If you cannot see and feel the difference between a market moving freely with conviction and one that is confused and chopping back and forth as the market pattern is unfolding, you do not understand it well enough to see any corrective pattern unfold in real time. In Figure 3.1 there are two bar charts of actual price data. Sample data '1' is intraday data from the S&P 500. Sample data '2' is a daily chart of a stock within the DJIA.

QUIZ: Study the data samples in boxes '1' and '2'. Find the stick diagram below the charts that best represents the actual price action in Figure 3.1.

STOP

■ ■ ■

The data in sample '1' is best described using line diagram 'C'. Many will pick 'A'. If you look more closely, all the line diagrams in 'A', 'B', and 'D' start with a down swing followed by an upswing that retraces *all* of the first down swing or exceeds it. That is the key. Only 'C' retraces just a portion of the first leg down and does not reach to prior high.

If you picked line diagram 'A', you likely set your comparison on the distance travelled by the first and last swings down. Both the first and last declining swings in the bar chart are of similar length, but diagram 'A' was intentionally drawn to catch you looking at the distance travelled rather than the special relationships between the three small swings in this correction.

If you put into practice the lessons of the first two chapters, the decline from '1' ends a five-wave pattern *higher* than the actual price low that ends the first swing. Figure 3.1b in the Exercise Appendix will show you where

FIGURE 3.1 Examination of Corrective Price Swings

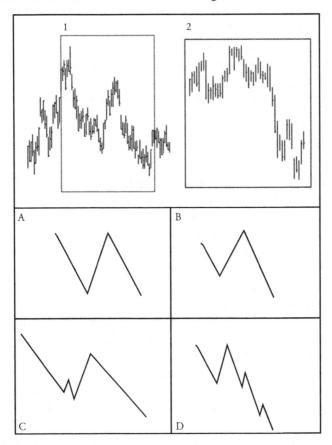

Source: Aerodynamic Investments Inc., © 1996–2012, Advanced Trading Seminar, www.aeroinvest.com.

the five-wave pattern ends. Then there is a bounce and a last swing down. This pattern loves to show up in markets with strong trends in the larger degree. The three-wave correction within box '1' was complete and soon new highs would follow.

Move on to sample data '2'. Both line drawing 'B' and 'D' are somewhat correct. Both represent the pattern unfolding, but neither will be perfect.

After a small pullback the market attempts a new high. It stalls for five bars failing under the same level of resistance. Up to this point both answers 'B' and 'D' are correct. The market then breaks down and creates a five-wave decline. Or does it? A beginner will see five waves down in sample '2' because you are only looking at the swings! It is a place to begin. A novice can pick answer 'B' or 'D' as they are correct for your level. If you knew answer 'B' was acceptable because the decline could be drawn as a simple line, that was great, but notice answer 'B' in the last leg down has not fallen as far below the last low as the actual market.

All these points are visual comparisons of proportion. If you have never done this before it is just a question of learning where to look. In the past we always asked, do you see it? We then assumed you do and it comes unglued with the first application.

What are we really looking for in these data samples?

Consider the following:

- Can you isolate three price swings? The middle leg can exceed the length of the first swing. At first we are not concerned where waves end and if the ending of the wave and swing is at the pivot. Just use the work you did in the Introduction to connect price swing to price swing.
- Does the middle swing overlap the first *entirely* when it tries to resume the larger trend and fails?
- Does the middle swing retrace only a portion of the first leg? (This point and the previous one are extremely important.)
- Can you see a five-wave pattern in the first swing? (If you do, you will immediately know what correction is developing when we cover it.)
- Can you see a complete five-wave pattern in the last leg? (All but one corrective pattern ends in this manner.)
- How would you describe the length in the first leg compared to the length of the third? Are they the same? Is the first much shorter than the last? Is the last leg longer?
- Have you looked in the prior trend to find the range of the previous fourth wave?
- Has your correction moved into this range?

If the data samples in '1' and '2' were apples and pears on a table, you would be learning how to draw them. You are learning how to look at their differences in shape and form within a confined space. That is what this is all about. Now let me get very particular and detailed. You learned in the last chapter to start counting waves developing five-wave structures *from the middle*. Do not stop now just because the chapter has moved your focus to corrective moves! Sample data '2' is best described using line graph 'D'. Answer 'B' does not fall far enough below the prior price low, even if you knew a straight line could represent the third swing down without more detail. Answer 'D' is proportionally a much better pick. In addition, if you made an error and thought sample '2' contained the same five-wave pattern down in the last swing as the line diagram, answer 'D' would most certainly be the best match. But using the skills we began to apply in Chapter 2, you will recognize that data sample '2' is an incomplete five-wave pattern down in the last swing. You counted swings again and not waves if this surprises you. Take a look at Figure 3.1b in the Exercise Appendix. That is a perfect example of why I always start these in the middle of the strongest leg down.

One line diagram is more detailed than the other, but both show us a market that attempts a new high and then breaks down below the price low to the left. Both are correct, but one is better. All of these corrective patterns we will be studying require this much attention to detail. I came to the realization most people are self-taught and the majority of books on any subject provide you with big picture examples. Your eye has been trained to see big and not innuendos.

A Zigzag Corrective Pattern

A Zigzag Corrective Pattern is the puzzle piece I captured for Figure 3.1 in data sample 1.

Figure 3.2 is a monthly chart of Apple stock displayed as a bar chart on the left and as a Japanese candlestick chart on the right. Study the correction within the white boxes. Though bar charts and candles are shown side-by-side, they should both have the same corrective feel to you. The first swing down is followed by a move that cannot retrace the entire path of the first. It fails to make a new high at that time and then the third swing down breaks the lows of the first. The third leg in the pattern travels a longer distance than the first. There is an abrupt ending and the larger uptrend resumes with conviction. The entire picture of the correction for Apple stock is a fast three-wave correction in a market creating a very strong bullish rally. That's where and how these types of corrections develop most often. The move that follows this correction is so powerful it is a good bet that the correction in Figure 3.2 was a second-wave decline leading to an extending third-wave rally.

In Figure 3.2 wave 'A' is a simple five-wave pattern. How do I know? It can be defined with three bars and not break any rules. Wave three is not the shortest. Wave four within 'A' does not overlap the first wave. On the other hand, wave 'C' is an extending five-wave pattern. Do you have to know this substructure detail to recognize a zigzag pattern? No because the middle leg in position 'B' cannot fully retrace the first leg.

Zigzag corrective patterns develop most often when strong trends become over-extended and they create fast reactions before getting on with

FIGURE 3.2 AAPL, Monthly

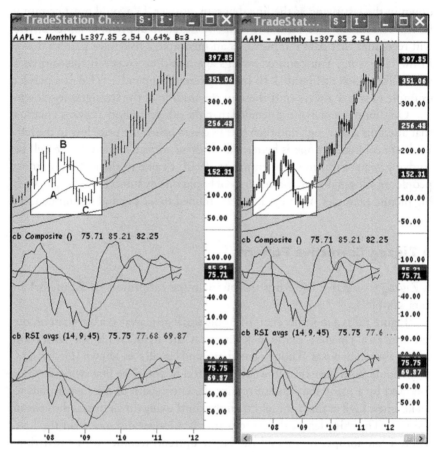

Source: Aerodynamic Investments Inc., © 1996–2012, Advanced Trading Seminar, www.aeroinvest.com; TradeStation.

the larger trend. But it is not always this easy to see their internals within the swings. This chart is so perfect it is a classic example. But you do not have to see these corrections in such clear detail as fuzzy internals cannot disguise the pattern that is unfolding.

Zigzag patterns *always* develop a five-wave swing in the first leg of the correction. Always? Well, there is one snag. We have not talked about five-wave patterns that create wedges and they create overlapping internal swings. They are viewed as legal patterns, but are rare. We will cover leading wedges later.

This is when my own students begin to feel pressure to understand. I know the question. It fits something like this: "But you said, impulse waves are always five-wave moves, are they not?" Now you are discussing completed five-wave patterns again.

Here is the point you could be missing. The five-wave pattern will complete the impulse wave. *But a correction that begins with a five-wave move is never complete.* It can never stand alone and start a sustainable move in the direction of the larger trend. Therefore one corrective pattern, the zigzag, begins with a five-wave pattern in the opposite direction of the larger trend, and we know immediately that it is only one leg within a developing three-legged correction.

The third leg in a zigzag will also define a five-wave pattern. In fact, all the corrective patterns, except for one type, will have a last leg that subdivides into five complete waves.

That is an area that causes some people trouble as well and raises another question. "How can a five-wave pattern define the last move in most corrections?" Do not forget it will *always* be the third and last leg leading to the end of the correction.

A much better question to ask is this. How do you know the zigzag pattern in Figure 3.2 is not the start of a new extending impulse wave down? Could the pattern be labeled waves (1) down, (2) up, and wave 1 of (3) down? That is a valid wave interpretation. But that is where I personally have a serious problem with people who only use wave structure to label charts. I detest computer interpretations, and refuse to develop Elliott Wave patterns in isolation. As an example, look at the oscillators in Figure 3.2 that align with the zigzag correction. RSI has fallen to about a range level of 40. Read *Technical Analysis for the Trading Professional, Second Edition.* I identify how the RSI will bottom in bull trends in a range of 40 to 45. Then notice how my Composite Index is diverging with the price lows and the RSI. This is a monthly chart. You would also look at the weekly chart and would find the same setup. Therefore, with confidence you know this is a corrective pattern unfolding and not the start of a new trend that will move in the opposite direction. This is just an introduction that shows how oscillators can be invaluable guides for us. We will devote a lot of time to using oscillators to help develop wave interpretations in the second book.

I hope that you are coming to the realization that five-wave swings will be found in the larger trend and counter-trend moves, but they carry a different message. When the corrective pattern starts with a five-wave structure, only one type of pattern can develop; that will be a zigzag. Therefore, in APPL's monthly chart the first leg down is a dead giveaway of the road map yet to come. We like these patterns a lot because you can trade them counter-trend and then they respectfully give clear entry levels to step back into the larger trend.

FIGURE 3.2a   A Corrective Zigzag Pattern Exercise

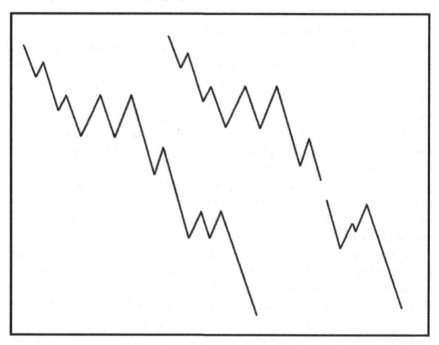

Source: Aerodynamic Investments Inc., © 1996–2012, Advanced Trading Seminar,
www.aeroinvest.com, TradeStation.

*In a zigzag there is always a middle bounce that does not retrace the full
path travelled in the first leg of the correction.* The middle leg can develop any
of the legal corrective patterns we are about to identify and study. But the
middle puzzle piece will be a complete corrective pattern that could stand on
its own as a sample of any one of the corrective patterns we are learning
about. In corrections we use letters to name the completed waves so they are
clearly defined as corrective units within the bigger picture. All three letters
must be placed near the end of their specific wave. The first wave is called
'A', the middle is marked 'B', and the last is 'C'. In Figure 3.2 a short-lived
simple bounce created wave 'B'. You will find triangles and other patterns
within wave 'B' that require more time to develop. But you can expect the
middle leg to be a smaller puzzle piece when compared to the entire
finished correction. It is a smaller pattern because it is a correction within
the larger correction. It must abide by all the rules that define any corrective
three-wave pattern. Therefore, wave 'B' up in Figure 3.2 could have defined
its own little zigzag. But in this case it did not. How do I know? You will as
well when this example comes back later in this chapter.

This is a good place to check your understanding. Keep in mind the last leg in the zigzag correction is always going to create a five-wave pattern. The first leg is always going to be a five-wave pattern. I suggest using boxes to enclose the first and last five waves. You have two zigzag patterns to label in Figure 3.2a. Mark the first ending as wave 'A' and mark the last wave 'C'. You know wave 'C' begins from where wave 'B' must end. Therefore you do not need to know the name of the pattern that creates 'B' and connects the first and third legs down. But if you can, that would be awesome as we have seen it in the second chapter and will study it next in detail. All right; give it a go now and see how well you do with the quiz in Figure 3.2a.

STOP

The answer will be found in the Exercise Appendix in Figure 3.2b.

The first five-wave pattern enclosed in the upper box of Figure 3.2b is the easiest to recognize. That was a simple five-wave pattern. Then you had to use your skills to create a completed five-wave pattern that extended. One might have been more difficult than the other for you to do.

In the second box of the first zigzag decline that does not have a gap, did you remember that all corrections will have three legs to define them? Wave '4 of C' looks just like the correction that connects these two five-wave patterns. It is the 'N' pattern we keep running into called a *flat*. If you put wave '5 of C' at the bottom of this middle leg that creates the 'N', you gave no consideration to the length of waves '1 of C' and '3 of C'. Plus your fifth wave did not break below the end of wave '3 of C'. That can happen, but we call it a failure.

The second zigzag in Figure 3.2a has a gap in the third wave that defines a five-wave pattern. The gap is a dead giveaway of where the middle of the move is for the last leg down. That's the point of recognition where everyone is on the same side of the market. Wave '4 of C' is its own private zigzag. They come in all sizes.

Figure 3.3 defines a very sharp correction in the Silver market. This weekly chart shows a sharp three-wave swing to a price target derived from Fibonacci analysis. Is it the bottom of a zigzag pattern? It is a complete pattern. This chart has been captured in real time. I'll let you be the judge of how well this pattern followed through with the message that the larger rally is incomplete.

The larger box that defines the market high was in fact drawn in the year 2010 when prices had not traded above $26. Now this market is at the critical juncture once again. The Composite is showing bullish divergence with the RSI. It warns the RSI is failing to detect a major trend reversal. We have a recognizable Elliott Wave Pattern. We have a pattern into a major price support area within the vicinity of a previous fourth wave.

FIGURE 3.3 Silver Futures, Weekly

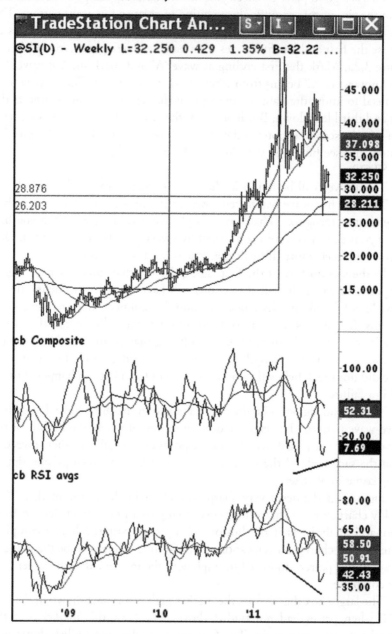

Source: Aerodynamic Investments Inc., © 1996–2012, Advanced Trading Seminar,
www.aeroinvest.com; TradeStation.

Notice how the middle leg of the corrective decline does not retrace the entire length of the first leg down. The third leg is also sharp and is the length of the first. That happens often. A 1.618 relationship often develops in the third leg relative to the first leg as well. I need spend no further time to name this pattern. It is a zigzag as it meets all the criteria that describes such a pattern. An added bonus is the oscillator position in the Composite Index.

One of the difficulties as a beginner is to recognize patterns when they come in different sizes. Sometimes the orientation is a problem. You can see the pattern in a decline, but do not detect it within the opposite direction or understand why it is moving in an opposite direction.

Figure 3.4 is a weekly chart for Exxon Mobil stock. Within this chart are two boxes of similar size. The fact these two boxes are of similar size will cause a problem for you, but the real challenge is recognizing that both of these boxes contain valid corrective zigzag patterns. You need to think how it is possible to contain a corrective pattern in both boxes when one is moving in the same direction as the larger trend. *Completed corrections can only move in counter-trend directions.* So how do we explain the first zigzag pattern contained within the lower box?

A Flat Corrective Pattern

I like the chart in Figure 3.4 a lot because it is the perfect lead into the next pattern we are going to study. It also shows you how markets use the exact same puzzle pieces over and over again. Figure 3.4 contains two boxes with zigzag patterns within each. Figure 3.4a is the exact same chart slightly enlarged. The upper box moves counter-trend to the larger uptrend and is a complete corrective zigzag pattern. We see that the uptrend resumes without trouble from this pattern.

The lower box also contains a zigzag pattern. However, when the market attempted to resume the larger uptrend it failed. The lower zigzag pattern is the *middle leg within a larger correction.*

The zigzag moving in the direction of the larger trend is now contained in a larger box that creates the N formation we have seen several times before. It is called a *flat.* This particular flat just happened to use a zigzag puzzle piece to develop its middle leg.

We can use lowercase letters a, b, and c to show we know that it is a completed three-wave pattern. But we have to put the name of the swing as it relates to the larger pattern developing. Therefore the end of the rising zigzag is called wave 'c of B'. The larger degree will use capital letters. Therefore wave 'B' is the smaller counter-trending swing within the larger three-legged

FIGURE 3.4 XOM, Weekly

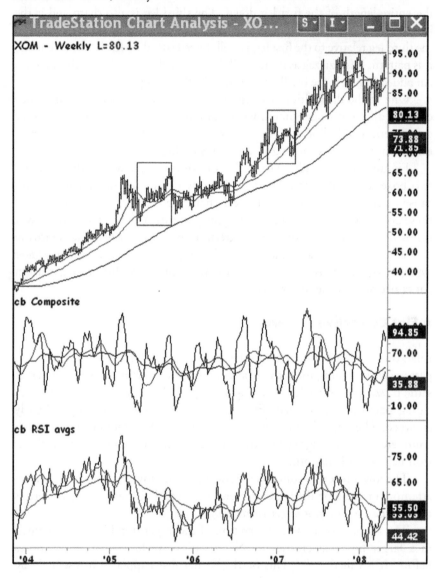

Source: Aerodynamic Investments Inc., © 1996–2012, Advanced Trading Seminar, www.aeroinvest.com; TradeStation.

correction. How far the market moves away from the resolution of wave 'B' will depend a great deal on where this middle leg ends compared to the extreme of the prior pivot that halted the larger trend. I know, that is a mouthful and it needs to be unpackaged for you.

FIGURE 3.4a Exxon Mobil (XOM) Weekly—Zigzag Patterns

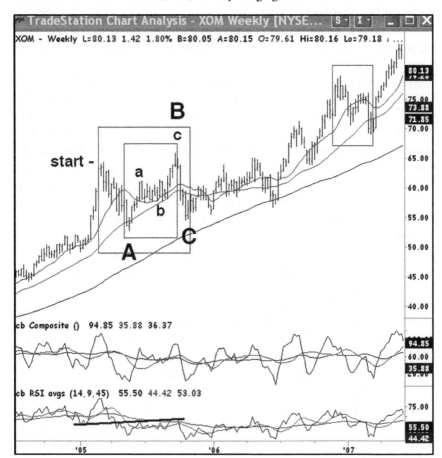

Source: Aerodynamic Investments Inc., © 1996–2012, Advanced Trading Seminar, www.aeroinvest.com; TradeStation.

Study Figure 3.4a and consider the pivot labeled 'start' to the end of wave 'c' of 'B'. From an old market top a correction develops defining wave 'A'. Pay attention to where wave 'A' began. Now look at the top of wave 'B'. Does the top of wave 'B' make a new high? You will likely say yes at first glance, but think about this answer. The ending of wave 'B' prints a trade higher than the start of wave 'A', but the market is only capable of creating a key reversal. A key reversal is a directional signal that carries the message that a trend has terminated. *I don't see a close above the old high.* So I would not view the last bar into the end of wave 'B' as a successful breakout. We then see a five-wave decline follow to create the third leg within the correction in the larger box that becomes wave 'C'.

When wave 'B' ends near the start of wave 'A', the target of the third leg will be to end the correction at the price level that marks the end of wave 'A'.

In this chart a five-wave pattern unfolds into the low marked wave 'C'. But wave 'C' does not carry all the way down to a price low that equals the end of wave 'A'. When the five-wave pattern within 'C' has all the sub-divisions needed to define 'C', and it ends short of the normal target, it is called a *running correction*. It is an additional identifying label that is rarely seen in real time. In hindsight, what follows will clearly explain why the last leg fell short. In real time you know the correction is complete because the oscillators will tell you so and the internal five-wave structure within wave 'C' is fully satisfied. The larger trend that follows running corrections will demonstrate strength and staying power. This particular correction within Exxon Mobil leads to a rally that holds together for another couple of years.

If I am making a big deal where wave 'B' ends relative to the start of wave 'A', what other alternatives do we have to consider?

When wave 'B' makes a move through the start of wave 'A' it leads to a pattern we call an expanded flat. The expanded flat creates a much larger move within wave 'C'. Figure 3.1 was an expanded flat corrective pattern in sample data '2'. We will go back to this pattern in a moment once we have fully exhausted the examination of the flat pattern.

The books of Robert Prechter make a strong point that a flat corrective pattern must define internal subdivisions of 3-3-5 as the three legs develop. The truth is in real time the first leg of the correction can be difficult to determine if it has internal structures that fit a three- or five-wave pattern. It can be very close. In Figure 3.4a wave 'A' is a series of bars that overlap one another. That one is clear, since we know it cannot be a five-wave pattern with so many overlapping bars. Therefore, more often than not it is by elimination that we declare a wave to have three-wave internals. Do we really care? No. If it is a choppy mess it is a three-wave swing. Case closed. Move on. Wave 'B' is then a beautifully defined zigzag pattern. It's not a piece of art! Sell it. Then after wave 'C' develops, get out of the way as the eye of a hurricane is coming your way from the opposite direction.

When trading these I usually exit the trending position into the target extreme. I do not mean at the extreme, but into it, as I am more comfortable banking profits early. Then I have some neutral time to think about reversing. I have never been very good at taking the same position and flipping it. It is just a matter of staying within your own comfort zone.

An Expanded Flat Corrective Pattern

The key to early identification of expanded flat corrective patterns is the middle leg. Wave 'B' is a three-wave swing in a correction that has already begun, but may not have been detected in the first leg. However, once the second leg labors out a choppy mess or a recognizable corrective pattern, you know exactly what is ahead for that market. In Figure 3.5 wave 'B' is a zigzag pattern. This time you have to adjust your eye to a time horizon that will give you lots of detail because it is an intraday chart. Wave 'B' breaks out above the old Gold market high ('start'). Once wave 'B' was fully developed the market failed. I was able to pick this one out early in a real-time scenario

FIGURE 3.5 Gold Futures 120-Minutes

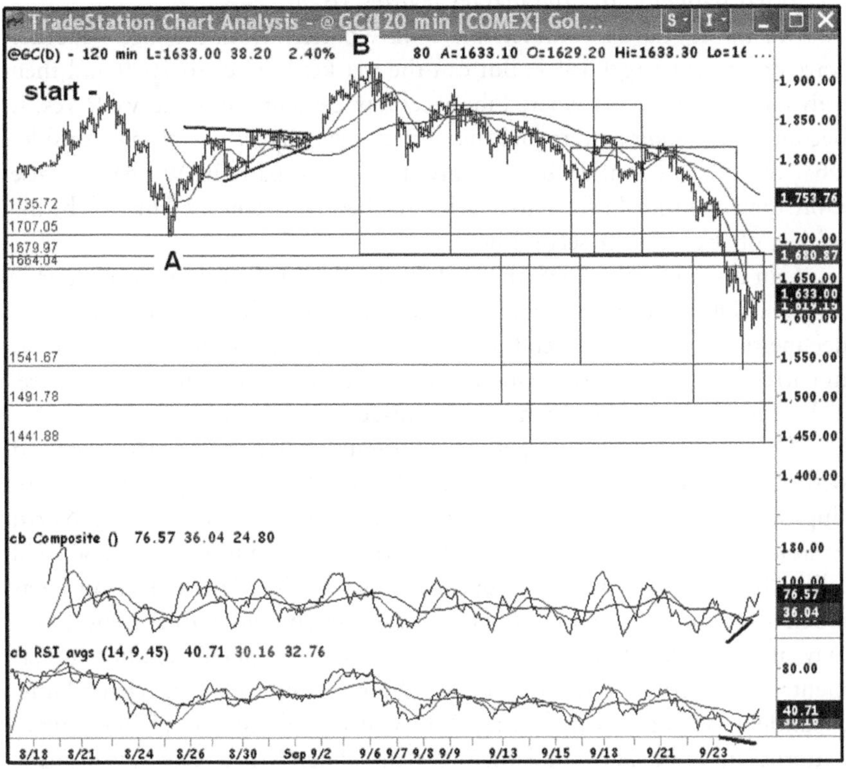

Source: Aerodynamic Investments Inc., © 1996–2012, Daily Market Report, www.aeroinvest.com; TradeStation.

because the middle leg within wave 'B' was a triangle. The triangle pattern we will discuss next. The 'C' wave declines that follow similar setups often extend with numerous subdivisions and always completing a five-wave pattern. In Figure 3.5 you can see where I defined the middle of the move near 1680. It is a horizontal level that divides the strongest leg down. All the boxes show equality swings above and below the midline. That's my way of keeping track of complex extending five-wave patterns. When I have as many boxes below the midline as above, the extending five-wave pattern is complete. These boxes are not enclosing five-wave patterns. It takes two boxes of equal size on either side of the midline to create an internal five-wave pattern.

Where is the target for wave 'C' going in the far right side of the chart?

About 1679, as that would mean the first and third legs would have travelled an equal distance. Sometimes the third leg may travel a 1.618 relationship to the first, but equality is normal when the decline is this strong.

What happens after the market realizes 1679?

We do not have a completed five-wave pattern from the high. Another wave down will target 1491. But can the market bounce to 1679 and then only fall to 1535–1541 where Fibonacci retracements cluster as well? Yes. It becomes a different pattern and that is precisely why we will always consider what options the market has for any developing pattern. We have to use more than one time horizon to develop the best wave counts. This will be the subject of study in the second book.

Can a swing from 1679 that falls to 1491 end the larger correction?

No. There needs to be another fourth wave rebound and fifth wave decline to complete an extending five-wave pattern. But do not forget that, in corrections, a five-wave swing cannot stand alone. It is only one of three. Take a look at another expanded flat correction in Figure 3.6.

This time a corrective pattern in Figure 3.6 is being demonstrated within a fundamental index called the Baltic Dry Index. It is the price to ship a ton of dry goods, mainly autos, across five shipping lanes to North America. As the economy weakens, the price to ship a ton of dry goods will fall. When the economy heats up, the cost will rise. This index can be as much as six months ahead of the general sentiment and market trends. You may also wonder if technical oscillators can be applied to other fundamental data series? Yes, with success. Single-family housing charts show expanded flat patterns unfolding. You will be able to find all these wave patterns in price and fundamental data alike. Why? The EWP maps human sentiment and we are a very predictable species in nearly everything we do.

FIGURE 3.6 Baltic Dry Index Monthly

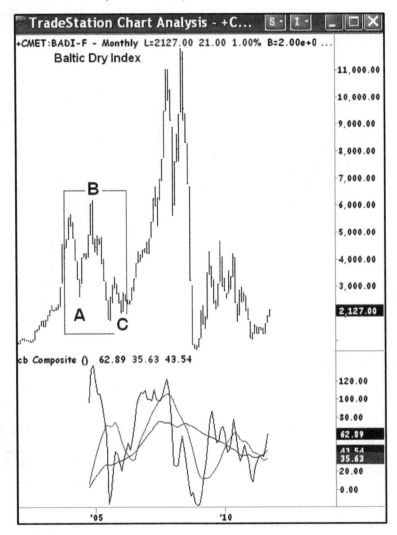

Source: Aerodynamic Investments Inc., © 1996–2012, Daily Market Report, www.aeroinvest.com; TradeStation, with CSI Unfair Advantage Data, www.csidata.com.

In Figure 3.7 we are looking at the USDJPY currency in weekly data. There are two corrective patterns captured within boxes.

The first correction is a very large zigzag that should be starting to become easier for you to recognize. It begins with a five-wave decline. It must therefore be incomplete after the first five-wave down and we know it

FIGURE 3.7 USDJPY Weekly

Source: Aerodynamic Investments Inc., © 1996–2012, Advanced Trading Seminar,
www.aeroinvest.com; TradeStation.

will become a zigzag pattern. Only zigzags have five waves within the first leg
of their corrective pattern. Then the rebound fails to retrace the entire
decline traveled by the first wave. The third leg down creates another five-
wave pattern.

The smaller correction in the second box to the right will be much harder for you. Is the correction an expanded flat pattern or is the box drawn too wide and the correct pattern is a zigzag rally? The real question you need to ask is: Is the *last swing up* in the smaller box a five-wave pattern or not? I think it is five waves. Therefore the box is drawn a little too far to the left so you can see the swings leading to an expanded flat correction. The actual low that starts the five-wave rally into the moving average has to be a 'B' wave because expanded flat patterns require wave 'B' to break the extreme of the prior trend. It is a failure. Figure 3.7b in the Exercise Appendix will show you how this structure developed.

You may not realize that the entire page becomes a massive expanded flat pattern. The last swing down is incomplete. The first and larger box enclosing a zigzag pattern is wave 'A' down in the larger pattern developing. Wave 'B' into the new high cannot create five waves. It must therefore be three. Eventually you will know the smaller patterns that connect this swing and push it into a new. But that will take time and practice. The oscillator double tops along with the market price high. Use more than one method to help you. Wave 'C' down then develops. It will be declining for many years.

When you are just starting it is really difficult to shift your focus from big picture to small and realize you have the same puzzle piece on your screen. The message the pattern carries does not change regardless.

Study the corrective pattern in Figure 3.8 marked wave '2' up. Can you see it too is an expanded flat? The way to learn Elliott Wave patterns is to hunt for just one type of pattern in various markets and different time horizons. It is best to study markets you favor and ones you have never looked at before. All markets serve to train our eye on how these patterns develop and how some markets develop slightly different characters, though the internals are all similar.

Make sure you examine bull and bear market trends. I always find bear markets easier to read. But we have to work on becoming proficient on both sides of the market. The only box in Figure 3.8 is a projection from the middle of the strongest move and equality proportional measurements from the midline to the high and then repeated from the midline to a new low. It shows I consistently use this method to help maintain balance as the market develops new swings.

Before leaving this introduction to expanded flat patterns, it cannot go without mention that they were once called irregular B patterns by Robert Prechter. The name was changed as they have nothing "irregular" about them and you will see these patterns develop in financial markets more often than their cousins the flat. But from this first name for this pattern came an industry

FIGURE 3.8   GE, Weekly

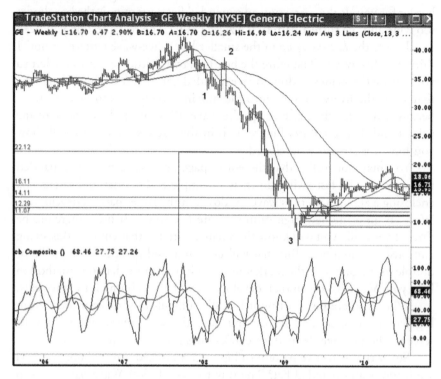

Source: Aerodynamic Investments Inc., © 1996–2012, Daily Market Report, www.aeroinvest.com; TradeStation.

slang that was never part of the Elliott vocabulary. The 'irregular B' never existed. There is no such animal. The implication being made by this slang term is the fact that the middle leg, or wave 'B', exceeds the origin of wave 'A'. That does not make the 'B' wave irregular. The name *irregular flat* referenced the entire pattern. So if you picked up this bad habit from someone, please stop using 'irregular B' in your discussion of the Wave Principle.

The Triangle Corrective Patterns

Triangles are the most misunderstood patterns of all. However, people continue to believe these are the easiest patterns to identify because they only look at the outer trend lines. If you follow that assumption you will get into a lot of trouble fast.

Figure 3.9 beautifully demonstrates two different markets producing triangle corrections. The upper left price chart displays a contracting triangle. The lower left chart is an expanding triangle.

If you never looked at the inside construction of these patterns you would simply note the contracting triangle is a coiling pattern of five overlapping swings. The bottom right line diagram is how the majority of novice wave practitioners would view the top left triangle. It does create five swings. Each price swing is a lower high or higher low with waves labeled a-b-c-d-e. Waves a-c-e might end at the same horizontal price level making

FIGURE 3.9 Contracting and Expanding Triangles

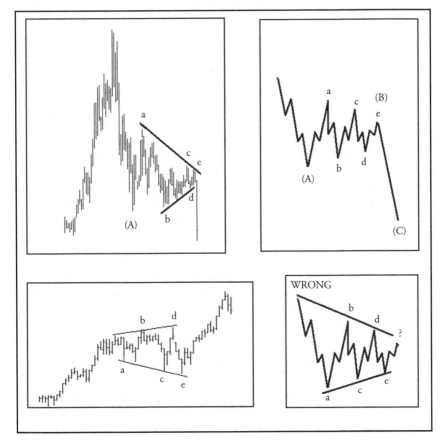

Source: Aerodynamic Investments Inc., © 1996–2012, Advanced Trading Seminar, www.aeroinvest.com; TradeStation.

the pattern look like a flat line on one side. But there is a massive error within this traditional view of triangle patterns.

1. None of the waves defining a triangle can be a five-wave pattern that stands alone. *Do not* label the first swing in a coiling pattern that is a five-wave structure as wave 'a' within the triangle. No exception, even though that price swing fits beautifully within the converging outer trend lines that appear to define it.
2. Triangles do not appear alone in second-wave positions.

QUIZ: If the first wave down is a five-wave pattern that stands alone, like the actual chart data in Figure 3.9 on the top left, what corrective pattern must be forming? (There is only one corrective pattern that begins with a five-wave pattern.)
STOP

■ ■ ■

The zigzag is the *only* pattern that begins with a five-wave structure. It is only one leg of three. If a correction looks like a contracting triangle, but the first swing is a clear five-wave pattern, you are creating a zigzag. Therefore the triangle is the middle leg and its resolution will be in the opposite direction from your expectations drawn in the bottom right of Figure 3.9.

The top left chart in figure 3.9 defines a five-wave pattern. It becomes wave (A). Then a contracting triangle follows and you can see that every swing within the triangle pattern cannot make a five-wave structure. Therefore they must be three-wave structures if you know their names or not. When we draw these as line figures we all tend to space waves a-b-c-d-e about the same. You can see in the real-life data this is not true. Expect wave 'c' within the triangle to take the most time or be the nastiest. They tend to chop and twist and turn traders on both sides of the market. The last swing in the top left shows waves 'c' and 'e' ending as two key reversals and rather close relative to the positions of 'a', 'b', and 'c'. That's all right. But what we fail to make clear in our line representations of a triangle is the fact that *each wave within a triangle will likely define a different corrective pattern*. My line diagram at the top right shows each swing as a zigzag. That's not likely to happen. It just makes it easy for me to draw it. But in real life wave 'a' within a triangle might be a zigzag followed by an expanded flat. There is a pattern alternation that often forms. They are the patterns we have covered.

It is very possible wave 'e' will create its own little triangle as its puzzle piece within the larger. These are all the reasons why triangles are tough to trade. The safest place is to trade the resolution or failure from the pattern.

The real market pattern on the top right of Figure 3.9 is a zigzag correction with wave 'B' defining a triangle. When it is complete the third leg of the corrective pattern must follow.

How many waves will develop out of the triangle? Five. Wave (C) down out of a triangle must produce a five-wave pattern. It is the definition of a zigzag.

QUIZ: If all corrective patterns ending with wave C create a five-wave pattern in wave 'C', can it be said all wave 'C's are five waves?

Think about this before reading on as it is very important.

STOP

■ ■ ■

The answer is no, because triangles have wave 'c's in their third swing and all swings within a triangle must be three-wave structures.

QUIZ: Can waves 'd' and 'e' be used in any other structure identified as an Elliott Wave pattern? What about a wedge?

STOP

■ ■ ■

The answer is no. Not even in a wedge do we use the letters 'd' and 'e'. The swings identified as waves 'd' and 'e' will only be seen within contracting and expanding triangles.

The traditional price objective derived from contracting triangles is to extend the trend line from 'b' behind the figure, so you can measure the height from 'a' to the opposite trend line. That measurement is then projected from the ending of wave 'e'.

I prefer not to extend the trend line behind 'b' and just measure the height of 'b' to 'a' as a right-angled projection. In other words, use the vertical rise and not the slope of the move. It is a more conservative target and that makes it safer. (In the final reading I recognized the need for clear examples of price projections from triangles. I will do this in the second book for you.)

The bottom left price chart in Figure 3.9 is an *expanding triangle*. This pattern is becoming of paramount importance in the United States today. See Figure 3.10.

Since 1999 the DJIA has been tracing out an expanding triangle pattern. The DJIA is close to ending wave (D) up. It is not perfect, you may state. It would be a failure if it ended here. I know stocks like Apple have incomplete

FIGURE 3.10 Dow Jones Industrial Average, Monthly

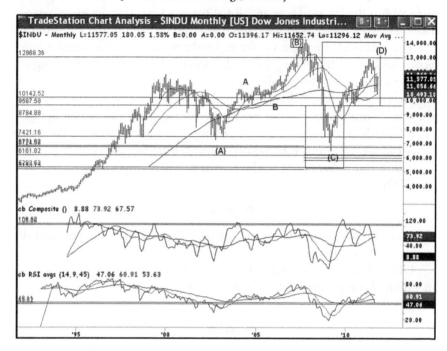

Source: Aerodynamic Investments Inc., © 1996–2012, Daily Market Report, www.aeroinvest.com; TradeStation.

rallies, but there is an index few monitor that is a cause of great concern. Gann timing points to March 2012 as a top. One index has done so already.

In Figure 3.11 the monthly chart for the S&P 500 Equal Weighted Index shows the second high exceeds the prior top. Most would call this a classic double top. In comparison, the Cash S&P 500 looks more like the DJIA in Figure 3.10. The last pivot top is far below the old high.

Never look at wave structure by itself. If it is a simple stock scenario, use a time horizon ratio of 4:1 to view two charts. If you study one stock, look at the top eight in its sector to see if it is tracking or alone.

In this example, the pattern being proposed in Figure 3.10 carries a devastating message. To hold on to this interpretation you know it would be seen in many global indexes. That is reason why, in the second book, we will learn how to increase the probability of our work by using other markets.

If wave (D) fails to press higher than (B) we would call it a failure just as we would when a fifth wave in a developing five-wave pattern fails to break above the extreme ending of wave '3'. But you will recall the fifth wave was required to complete a small five-wave structure as its last impulse wave.

FIGURE 3.11   S&P 500 Equal Weighted Index (left) and S&P 500 Cash Index, Monthly

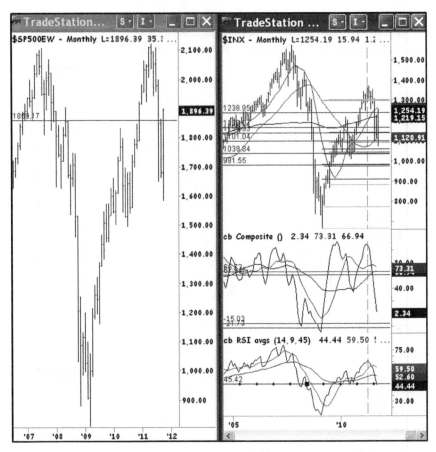

Source: Aerodynamic Investments Inc., © 1996–2012, Daily Market Report,
www.aeroinvest.com; TradeStation.

So too in this failure within the triangle. We need to build our basic skills
more to move into this more advanced application. But I have put a carrot
before you to help motivate you to slug onward with the basics.

I know these beginning steps can be dry when you have to learn the basic
puzzle pieces. But you know something? You made it. Every other puzzle
piece you must consider will combine the patterns we have already covered.

Before we move away from triangles, there are a few more points to learn.

Figure 3.12 contains a contracting triangle in a daily chart of the 30-year
U.S. Treasury bond. The tight back and forth price action near the end of
the contracting pattern is how the pattern looks when wave e defines its own
small triangle in the last swing.

FIGURE 3.12   U.S. 30-Year T-Bond Futures, Daily

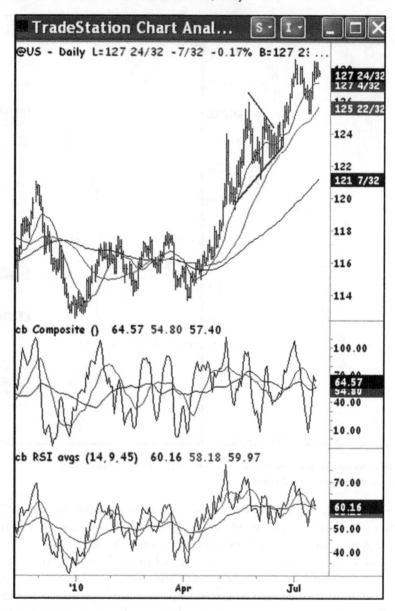

Source: Aerodynamic Investments Inc., © 1996–2012, Daily Market Report, www.aeroinvest.com; TradeStation.

Notice the price action out of this corrective pattern when the larger trend resumes. It is usually this strong and has a name. It is called the *thrust out of a triangle*. As triangles cannot develop as a standalone corrective pattern in a second wave position, this triangle is in a fourth-wave position.

FIGURE 3.13   BAC, Weekly

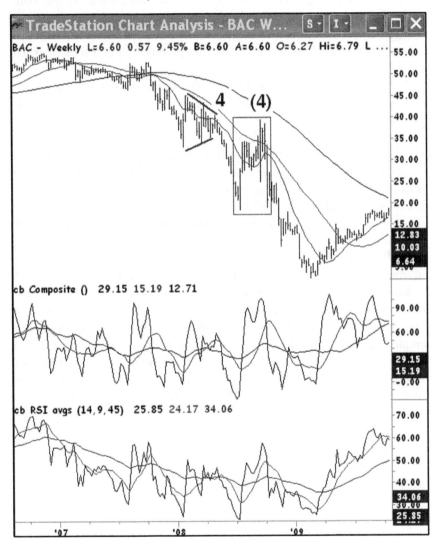

Source: Aerodynamic Investments Inc., © 1996–2012, Daily Market Report, www.aeroinvest.com; TradeStation.

That is very useful to know. We also know corrections retrace back to previous fourth waves. Therefore, when a chart may be difficult to interpret, look for the corrections that attract one another in fourth-wave positions.

In Figure 3.13 Bank of America stock offers a perfect example of back-to-back fourth waves. The first is a contracting triangle. The second is a zigzag. The second ends at the apex of the triangle pattern. Notice the thrust down from the triangle. This is the very common action that follows both contracting and expanding triangles.

Figure 3.13 is a classic back-to-back development of fourth waves. If you see this, it is a great place to start a wave interpretation. It is also useful when you do not have the historical data.

You are going to see contracting triangles far more often than expanding triangles. My 25-year career so far can name very few expanding triangle examples.

I would like to add for readers of my book, *Fibonacci Analysis,* that the only time the Fibonacci confluence zones are ignored by a market is when a triangle is developing. It is so consistently repeatable that I use it as an indicator by itself. If a market ignores my Fibonacci confluence calculations, look for the triangle as the market is rescaling. The thrust from the pattern creates a new price grid and the market returns to respecting all your calculations again.

Well, we did it! We have covered all the corrective patterns in the universe. Perhaps a better description is to state that we have covered all the basic building blocks to create any corrective pattern. We need to learn how to connect these basic formations together. We also need to learn a few more guidelines about markets that define complex patterns. But even complex patterns are just a string of these same basic patterns that group together to develop more time consuming corrections. Fortunately we can move that discussion about complex structures to a second book so you can develop your confidence now with the basic building blocks that are most productive to trade.

CHAPTER 4

Diagonal Triangles (Wedges)

Termination and Leading Patterns

Now that you have the start of a working vocabulary regarding corrective patterns, it will be easier to examine these wedge-shaped patterns in a more meaningful way. Then, when we have finished this discussion, you will be ready for your first exam to really anchor these concepts and to uncover any weaknesses you may have. In Chapter 5 is a practice exam to build your confidence. Then (also in Chapter 5) the final exam will follow to ensure you are starting to see the basic patterns. The second book, Advanced Elliott Wave Analysis: Complex Patterns, Intermarket Relationships, and Global Cash Flow Analysis, *will begin at the intermediate level. Do not move on to the Intermediate material until you are comfortable and know you are ready.*

Looking at the basic corrective patterns first was important because the internals of the most common diagonal triangle pattern uses these same corrective patterns to develop the larger wedge formation. There are two types of Diagonal Triangles and they carry very different messages.

Termination Diagonal Triangle Pattern

The Diagonal Triangle you will see most often brings a message of market trend exhaustion. It is running on fumes in the direction of the larger trend. The pattern has a wedge appearance and the internals of these patterns are *all* corrective patterns building upon one another.

As an example, Figure 4.1 was a Termination Diagonal Triangle that developed in the S&P 500 mini futures contract in a 60-minute time horizon. If your company saves intraday data, you will find this pattern in the data that developed from February 10 to February 22, 2011. Figure 4.1 is a classic example of these patterns, showing you that the resolution is a fast market retracement to the origin of the wedge pattern.

Below the actual market chart is a copy of the wedge with the impulse waves i, iii, and v all contained within their own boxes. The slope of each is

FIGURE 4.1 S&P 500 Mini Futures, 60 Minutes Forming a Diagonal Triangle

Source: Aerodynamic Investments Inc., © 1996–2012, Daily Market Report, www.aeroinvest.com; TradeStation.

easily compared by looking at an imaginary line running from the bottom left corner to top right corner. The slope falls forward in each box relative to the previous box.

The termination wedge follows the same guideline as developing triangles. Each wave must be a three-wave pattern, and you will often see them alternate in each wave as to the corrective pattern they display. In Figure 4.1 this wedge defines three corrective patterns within each box. The box to the left is an expanded flat. The 'B' is a failure as it did not fall below the ending of wave '4', which is also the start of wave 'a' in an expanded flat pattern. I am comfortable with this because the trend preceding this failure was so strong. If you believed the first small move up (above '4') is a five-wave pattern, you would call the move into the end of wave 'i' a zigzag pattern. You can see how different patterns might be used to describe a pattern and they do not change the end of the move or the outcome that follows. That is very important to understand. In the real world the market may hand you a structure that falls in a gray area when you have to label it. Use common sense. In this case, you would not know a termination wedge was about to occur from just the data that creates wave 'i' of 5. But you catch on very quickly when wave 'ii' is clearly a corrective choppy pattern. Wave 'iii' grinds onward and makes two new highs. All the choppy action and corrective swings warn that a rising wedge is under construction. The length of each bar is getting shorter and shorter, and some people might have considered the middle leg in wave 'iii' to be a distribution top. I do not use classic patterns such as distribution patterns because they have a low probability for giving guidance on when to execute the trade. But if you know enough to use the oscillator for guidance it is too soon to think the end will occur in the middle of wave 'iii' of 5. The use of oscillators will be covered in a higher skill level.

Consider the middle box far more closely. Within the middle box there is a swing up followed by a choppy sideways stall, followed by a small thrust up from the chop to end wave 'iii' of 5. This is where many people are drawn in too early to execute trades for the decline to come. They label the first swing up as wave 'iii', the sideways price chop as wave 'iv', and the last move up as wave 'v'. They try to fit all the required waves—'iii', 'iv', and 'v'—into the middle box. But if you know about the slope comparison between impulse waves 'i', 'iii', and 'v', you would know the top right corner of the middle box is only the end of wave 'iii'. Then a correction that is shallow develops and that leads to the third box. Inside this third box we have a contracting triangle. The market has exhausted the upward trend and the reaction is strong and swift as a counter-trend move unfolds.

Where is the safest place to enter an order to sell this market? It is not anywhere within the wedge. If you try to catch the top you could be forced to stay out of the counter-trend move because your losses are so large from stepping in several times prematurely. When the move finally occurs, which you had anticipated, you are wounded on the sidelines with no entry level of low risk to step in. Don't be the guy who has to hold the top ticket for the move. There are no bonus chips for being first. That took me years to learn when I was just beginning. You think you want to be first so you can just sit there and enjoy the ride. A safer place is to sell as the market stalls *under* the lower trend line of the wedge for several hours. The truth is you do not know if the pattern is complete because that small pullback that stalls under the trend line could have become wave 'iv' that creates its own triangle pattern. But the Composite Index under the data is telling me otherwise as it is topping at an old resistance level. That is why I apply all the methods that I have developed a familiarity with to build a wave interpretation. If I know a Gann target date, the time element will be more important than the pattern itself. If the date needed more time, an extension in the wave 'iv' position would have been favored. Whether you know these other methods of technical analysis or not, the message does not change what Elliott described for us. These wedges with overlapping internals that develop corrective patterns linked together are trend killers. Pay attention to them.

Diagonal Triangles love company. Figure 4.2 is slightly different than Figure 4.1. Follow both Cash and Futures, as the minor differences will help your entry timing. This is the same underlying market relative to the futures chart in Figure 4.1. But you may see wedges develop in T-Bonds, or metals, or other financial markets all at the same time. When you do see this you know something big is coming. Let's test your understanding of Diagonal Triangle patterns to this point.

QUIZ:

Is Figure 4.2 correct? Remember, every swing will create a complete corrective pattern.

STOP

■ ■ ■

Well, this example is incorrect. The first wave of the wedge has to start from the pivot low just to the left. A chart can be found in the Exercise Appendix in Figure 4.2a. The first wave of the wedge connects more than one basic corrective pattern. When this happens we call them complex corrections.

FIGURE 4.2 S&P 500 Cash Index, 120-minutes—A Diagonal Triangle with Pattern
Resolution

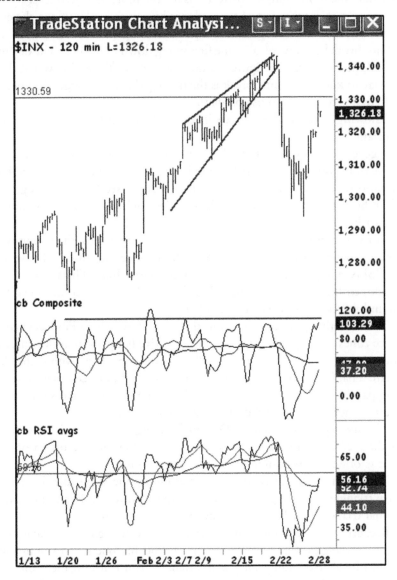

Source: Aerodynamic Investments Inc., © 1996–2012, Daily Market Report,
www.aeroinvest.com; TradeStation.

But they only use the same basic patterns we covered in Chapter 3. I am going to separate the more complex corrections for the more advanced levels.

The way to see the start of the wedge is by correctly identifying the end of wave 4. Wave 4 is an expanded flat pattern though wave 'c' in the last leg does not break below wave 'a' in the first swing down in the box. The decline that follows the wedge in Figure 4.2 does not retrace the entire wedge. The only way to know if the first break is the first leg down in a larger decline, or an alternate scenario is to use oscillators.

Knowing how a wedge appears in a slightly longer time horizon can be important.

Figure 4.3 returns to the S&P 500 futures mini contract in a 240-minute time horizon. The time horizon is four times that used in Figure 4.1. The ratio of 1-to-4 is important. In this chart we see how the wedge fits within the larger trend. We see a fifth wave developing from a flat correction that just has waves 'A', 'B', and 'C' identified.

At the top of wave 5 where the Diagonal Triangle ends, the Composite Index is showing bearish divergence to both the price data and the 14-period RSI. RSI is failing to detect the trend change approaching. This is the reason I developed the Composite Index. The formula has momentum imbedded in it and serves to show when RSI is failing.

The underlying support levels in the chart show where Fibonacci confluence zones offer strong support. The corrective flat pattern in this chart is a fourth wave and the decline has fallen to the top of 'B' within the flat pattern. That is why the bounce that follows is significant. But that rally is a zigzag pattern and the last swing down shows the market retraces the entire corrective zigzag. The larger decline was incomplete.

The message a termination Diagonal Triangle will carry is a warning that the trend will reverse. The reversal that follows to the origin of the wedge is often the beginning of a much larger move.

The internals are all corrective and abide by the same rule for a corrective triangle. No swing marked as a complete wave within a termination diagonal triangle may have a five-wave pattern on its own.

Because we have both contracting corrective triangles and expanding corrective triangles, I do wonder if R. N. Elliott has one pattern omission. It would be an Expanding Diagonal Triangle. You run into them on rare occasions and I have always been able to find an alternate way to label them using the patterns viewed as the complete set we have already examined. But is there a fourteenth pattern? If there is, the DJIA pattern in Figure 3.10 is a scary proposition on what that pattern message is describing for the years ahead. I favor wave (E) down in a large fourth wave. So the message is the

FIGURE 4.3   S&P 500 Mini Futures, 240-Minutes

Source: Aerodynamic Investments Inc., © 1996–2012, Daily Market Report,
www.aeroinvest.com; TradeStation.

same up to a point. But then a few hard questions will have to be considered in the years ahead when the DJIA stalls on support levels at 5100 to 5400 or 4500.

Leading Diagonal Triangle Pattern—Type 2

The Diagonal Triangle patterns that have corrective internals and occur at the exhausted conclusion of a larger trend are, without question, the type of wedge pattern you will encounter most often. But Robert Prechter Jr., in his book *Elliott Wave Principle*, describes a pattern R. N. Elliott mentions as Diagonal Triangle Type 2. There is not much on this pattern in most books, as it is not often encountered. But in hindsight, there will be times when the only way to describe a market move is to call upon the Type 2 Leading Diagonal Triangle pattern.

FIGURE 4.4 S&P 500 Cash Index, Daily

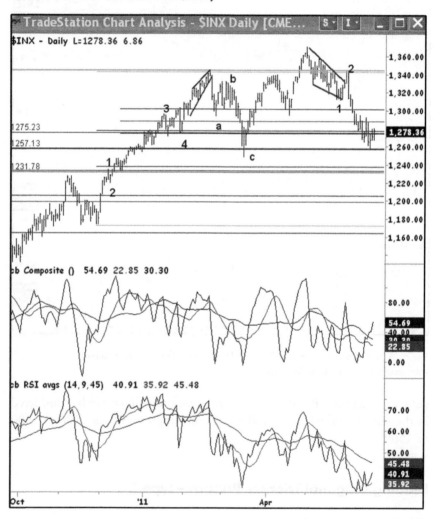

Source: Aerodynamic Investments Inc., © 1996–2012, Daily Market Report, www.aeroinvest.com; TradeStation.

These are sneaky so-and-sos that destroy the unaware. The market you will find them hiding in most often will be in Treasury Bond and all global fixed income markets, FOREX on occasion, but bonds bloom these patterns often. These are markets that love to stall and chop at trend reversals. Then all of a sudden a report is released and the new trend unfolds with conviction. The long periods of chop before the trend reversal becomes clear is what is so difficult to describe.

Figure 4.4 is very interesting as it is a type 2 diagonal triangle that defined wave 'A' up in a developing zigzag corrective rally. The wedge is very

FIGURE 4.5 S&P 500 Mini Futures, 22-Minutes

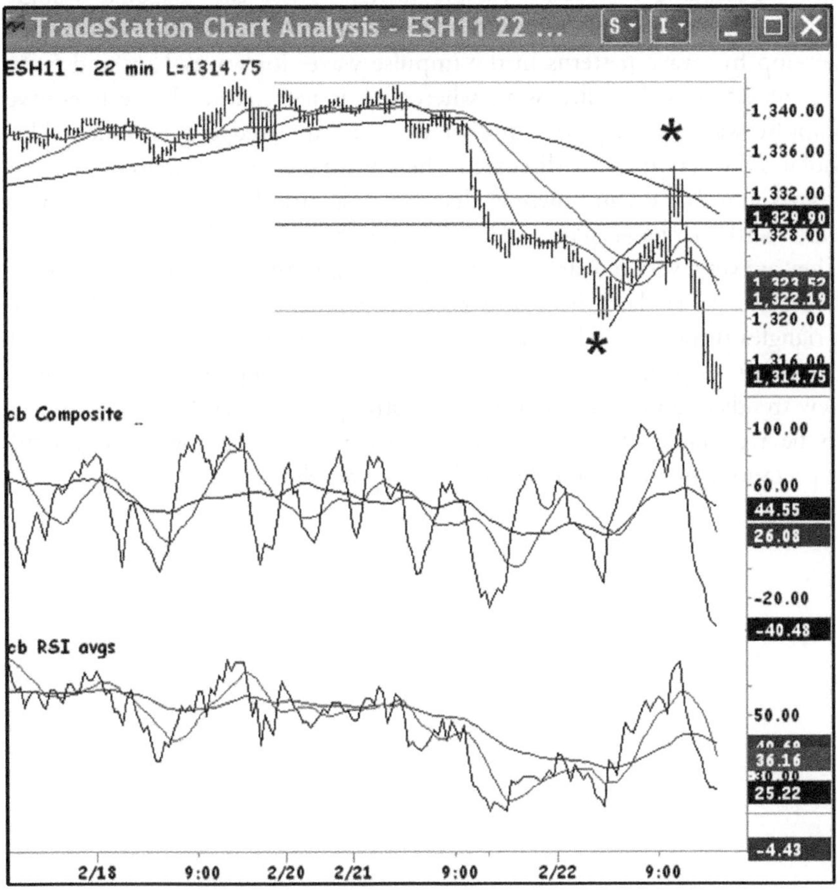

distinctive in this 22-minute March 2011 S&P 500 futures contract. They are found in wave 'A' and first wave positions *only*. (If that isn't an exam question hint, I don't know what else it could be!) The zigzag highlighted by the asterisk symbol (*) shows wave 'A' is the wedge that moves to the previous fourth wave to the left. The wedge is followed by a shallow decline that leads to a final swing up that likely short squeezed many day traders.

It does not matter whether I offer a long time horizon or a short intraday chart for you to examine. As in Figure 4.5, the patterns will always look very similar. They cannot be detected in real-time as they develop. They are revealed after the fact when the larger move becomes transparent.

How do you differentiate between the Termination Diagonal Triangle and the Leading Diagonal Triangle variety? These two diagonal triangle patterns have very different internal structures. The leading wedge will develop five-wave patterns in the impulse waves for waves 1, 3, and 5. In Figure 4.5 it is the third wave where this is most clear. These five-wave impulse waves overlap one another to create the wedge appearance. This violates the very rules we discussed where wave 4 cannot overlap wave 1. So it goes, life goes on and these wedges do exist, and there is no other way to describe the larger structure that follows without them. Don't abuse them! They are very, very rare and only recognized in hindsight in most cases. One book tries to explain the entire FOREX market using Leading Diagonal Triangles throughout. That is not using the Wave Principle. These are not patterns to explain the unknown, but they do develop at the beginning of new trends or zigzag corrections where strong moves develop. They appear to be repeatable in the exact same wave positions and have repeatable expectations in any time horizon that they develop.

CHAPTER 5

A Summary with Study Flash Cards for Patterns, Rules, and Guidelines

The time has come to test your understanding. If you move too quickly beyond the basics it is easy to develop bad habits that are difficult to change later. So this chapter will serve to find the weak spots and boost your confidence.

In this chapter, the first six figures are just corrective patterns from actual chart data. I have found small to very large patterns of the same kind to help you see how the size does not change the description of the pattern. We have studied corrective fats, expanded flats, zigzags, and triangles. All these basic patterns have been grouped into like patterns to help you learn. Expanded triangles do not develop that often. The best example can be examined in the current weekly or monthly DJIA that we discussed in Chapter 3. The method of putting boxes around a pattern is demonstrated, since this method will help you study your own charts in a similar way.

I spent considerable time hunting for the triangles that cause the greatest problems for people because they break in the opposite direction of how most people think they will resolve. The key is to ensure no leg has a five-wave pattern that stands by itself. The examples in this chapter show you what will happen if you forget this important point.

There are two different exams to help you. The first is a practice exam to shake out some of the common problems that people discover they missed. That gives you a chance to reread a section if needed. The second exam is the one you need to measure your understanding before you move on to the intermediate level in the second book. None of these questions is designed to *intimidate or trick you into a common pothole in the road. Besides, I want to reserve that right for when you get overconfident at the Master Level! So for now you are safe, and all the questions in this chapter have only one purpose—to build your confidence and plant a mile marker on our road of progress.*

Just one last point if you have more experience than I have covered in the beginner level. As you are aware, many more things can be said about corrections. But I am deliberately focusing on just the basics. Do not skip these exams. Most people I meet for coaching purposes have underlying errors or smaller points unknown that compound issues in more advanced work. You need to ensure your basic work is impeccable.

■ ■ ■

It helps to have a cheat-sheet when you do the exams in this chapter and to help you study before your computer. You can scan them and print them out or leave them on your computer for quick reference. Either way they have the basic patterns we have covered so far. In the next section I will add to your list of patterns so you can begin to see how these individual patterns can be used to develop more time consuming corrections.

Study Flash Cards for the Basic Patterns

These are the Elliott Wave Principle patterns we have studied so far:

1. A simple five-wave pattern.
2. An expanding five-wave pattern.
3. A failure fifth wave.
4. A termination diagonal triangle.
5. A leading diagonal triangle—type 2.
6. A *zigzag* corrective pattern.
7. A *flat* corrective pattern.
8. An *expanded flat* corrective pattern.
9. A *contracting triangle* corrective pattern.
10. An *expanding triangle* corrective pattern.

These 10 patterns are in fact the only patterns you need to learn. The intermediate level in the next book will combine these same patterns to explain more complex corrections. As an example the zigzag pattern will sometimes repeat and we then identify it as a double zigzag. But it will just be two zigzag patterns glued together. It is the connector 'x' that causes people the greatest trouble. For this reason I bumped all that more advanced discussion into the Intermediate graduate work.

Because the extending five-wave patterns are so difficult to know just where you are within them, I have a different chart style in Figure 5.1. It shows these extending patterns must end with a specific number of swings. The number of waves in an impulse wave is five.

FIGURE 5.1   CVX, Monthly

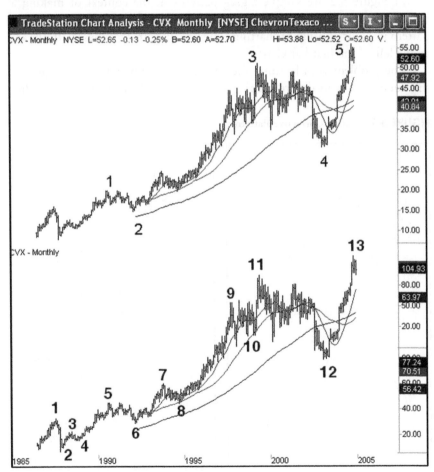

Source: Aerodynamic Investments Inc., © 1996–2012, Advanced Trading Seminar, www.aeroinvest.com; TradeStation.

If it extends further you must add another four swings in total, always adding a pair of swings in the front and a pair on the end. The first pair will become waves 1 and 2. The last pair must satisfy waves 4 and 5. Therefore, nine swings may end an extending five-wave pattern, but 9 plus 4 is 13. The series grows by the following set; 5, 9, 13, 17, 21, and so on. Figure 5.1 shows you conventional wave labels and then a continuous way to count waves. The only thing to keep in mind is to remember waves must be complete to label them. The number of swings is counted rather than the subdivisions using conventional Elliott notation. The point here is that 11 will never end an impulse wave. So count first; name patterns later.

In Figure 5.2 are sample zigzag patterns in the context of making a correction in bull and bear markets. The chart on the right is also a zigzag pattern in point-and-figure charting. The line diagrams for these patterns are to the left of the first bar charts.

The problem with learning the corrective wave patterns is recognizing the same pattern in different sizes. The internals all meet the criteria that

FIGURE 5.2 Zigzag Corrective Pattern

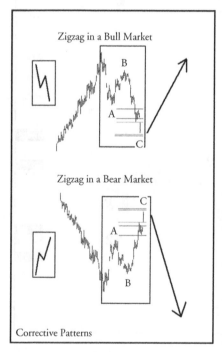

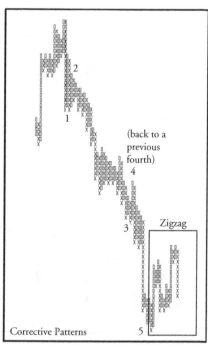

Source: Aerodynamic Investments Inc., © 1996–2012, Advanced Trading Seminar, www.aeroinvest.com; TradeStation.

FIGURE 5.3   Zigzag Corrective Patterns

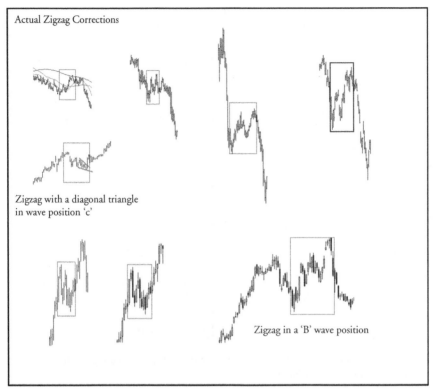

Source: Aerodynamic Investments Inc., © 1996–2012, Advanced Trading Seminar, www.aeroinvest.com; TradeStation.

define the specific pattern, but then the person learning is unable to see the pattern when the size changes. Therefore, Figure 5.3 offers examples copied directly from market charts of various time horizons. Learn to recognize the feel of the pattern more than a set of rules.

The expanded flat is far more difficult to learn than the Flat. In Figure 5.4 the expanded flat that developed in the S&P 500 is perfection. But do not expect such clarity in all situations.

Figure 5.5 has captured various expanded flats and flats so you have a reference card of various markets and time horizons to compare. They all demonstrate these patterns in various ways. As an example, there is an expanded flat within a 'B' wave position that is within a larger corrective pattern we know as a flat. This is a good introduction to what we will be developing for you when we begin the intermediate material in the next

FIGURE 5.4   Flat and Expanded Flat Corrective Patterns

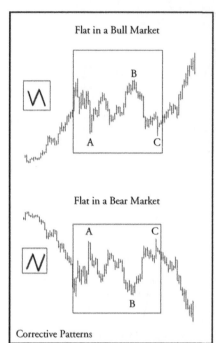

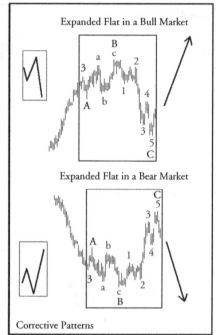

Source: Aerodynamic Investments Inc., © 1996–2012, Advanced Trading Seminar, www.aeroinvest.com; TradeStation.

book, *Advanced Elliott Wave Analysis: Complex Patterns, Intermarket Relationships, and Global Cash Flow Analysis.*

Some of these patterns require many bars to develop and some need minimal bars to be correctly identified, since they all carry the same look. It will not take you long to know these patterns if you study short horizon charts. That way you have the opportunity to study many patterns in shorter periods of time. Scroll from the older date forward. Do not try to call the pattern in real time to start. That is beyond the basic skill level you have for just for a short while.

Figure 5.6 gives you actual market data for the corrective patterns we call contracting triangles. Particular care has been given to find the triangles that our industry often identifies incorrectly. That is when the first leg in the coiling pattern is five waves by itself. That is not where the triangle begins. It starts in the next swing. All corrections that begin with five waves will develop into zigzag patterns. Therefore these triangles fall within wave 'B' as the middle leg of the larger zigzag corrections.

FIGURE 5.5 Flat and Expanded Flat Corrective Patterns

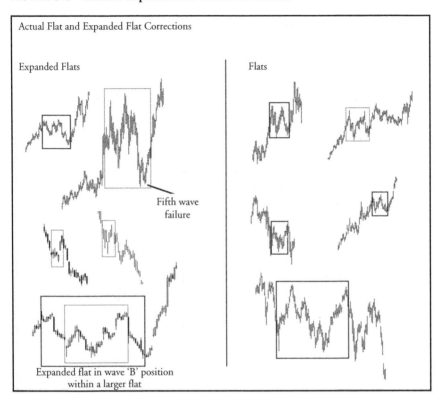

Actual Flat and Expanded Flat Corrections

Expanded Flats

Flats

Fifth wave failure

Expanded flat in wave 'B' position within a larger flat

Source: Aerodynamic Investments Inc., © 1996–2012, Advanced Trading Seminar, www.aeroinvest.com; TradeStation.

A Summary of Rules and Guidelines

The patterns have been listed for you to study. Now we need to summarize the rules and guidelines. Again, these may not be all of them, but for a beginner level they are complete.

Rules

Impulse Waves:

1. Wave 3 may not be the shortest as compared to impulse waves 1, 3, and 5. This does not mean wave 3 has to be the longest.

FIGURE 5.6 Contracting Triangle Corrective Patterns

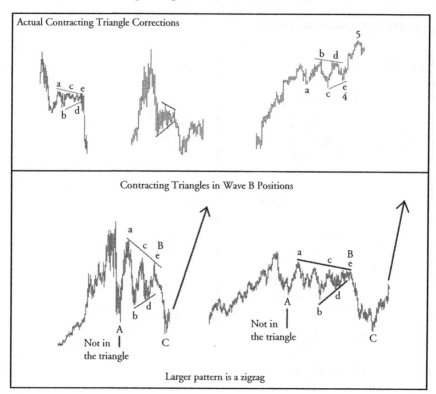

Source: Aerodynamic Investments Inc., © 1996–2012, Advanced Trading Seminar,
www.aeroinvest.com; TradeStation.

2. Wave '2' may not retrace beyond the distance travelled in wave '1'.
   Another way to say this is wave '2' cannot break the start of wave '1'.
3. Wave 4 may not overlap any part of the distance traveled by wave 1. There
   is one exception: the very rare leading diagonal triangle, type 2, that serves
   as the first impulse wave in a new trend or counter-trend move. This is
   rarely encountered outside the Treasury markets.
4. Every impulse wave must contain an internal wave structure that subdivides into a separate and complete five-wave pattern.
5. *All* corrective patterns that end with wave 'C' will develop an internal
   substructure of a five-wave pattern. (Triangles do not end at wave 'C',
   explaining why triangles do not follow this rule.)

Guidelines

Corrective Waves:

1. Corrective waves are attracted to the previous fourth wave of one lesser degree. Think of this as fourth waves tend to come together within the same area of your chart.
2. When a simple pattern develops in a wave '2' position, a more complex pattern that combines patterns may develop in the wave '4' position. This is known as the guideline of alternation. If wave '2' is complex the fourth wave may develop a simple pattern.
3. Corrective waves of the same degree have a proportional guideline. If the correction developing takes 2.618 times longer than the comparable correction, it is likely not a correction in the same degree. In other words, wave 'ii' and wave 'iv' will be related in time and size to an extent. If suddenly wave 'iv' has taken three times that needed to create wave 'ii', then you likely are defining wave '4' in the next larger degree and not wave 'iv'. The market is farther ahead than your favored scenario indicates.
4. Markets that create back-to-back repeating patterns of the same kind, but the repeating pattern is getting smaller and smaller each time, are warning you that the coiling repeated corrections will produce a strong spectacular move.
5. Triangles, both contracting and expanding patterns, are the only patterns allowed to use the identifying labels 'd' and 'e'. They cannot be used within wedges. They cannot be used in complex extending impulse waves. They are never found as a means to connect two patterns together.
6. Triangles are not found in second wave positions by themselves. They can be in 'B' wave positions, but not as the only pattern.
7. Every wave within a triangle must be a three-wave structure.
8. Wave 'c' in zigzags will often travel a distance that is 1.618 that traveled by wave 'a' within the pattern.
9. Termination diagonal triangles will have slopes that flatten in each impulse wave compared to the prior impulse wave.

A Table of Degree Labels and Names

The table in Figure 5.7 shows how we label charts to show the fractal properties of waves. The corrective patterns that need a connector in more complex and time-consuming counter-trend moves will use 'x', 'y', and 'z'.

FIGURE 5.7   Conventional Degree Notation

Grand Supercycle	Ⓘ	Ⓘ	Ⓘ	Ⓘ	Ⓥ	Ⓐ	Ⓑ	Ⓒ
Supercycle	(I)	(II)	(III)	(IV)	(V)	(A)	(B)	(C)
Cycle	I	II	III	IV	V	A	B	C
Primary	①	②	③	④	⑤	Ⓐ	Ⓑ	Ⓒ
Intermediate	(1)	(2)	(3)	(4)	(5)	(A)	(B)	(C)
Minor	1	2	3	4	5	A	B	C
Minute	ⓘ	ⓙ	ⓘ	ⓙ	ⓥ	ⓐ	ⓑ	ⓒ
Minuette	(i)	(ii)	(iii)	(iv)	(v)	(a)	(b)	(c)
Subminuette	i	ii	iii	iv	v	a	b	c

plus X, Y, and Z in all degrees for complex corrections and D, E for triangles

Source: Elliott Wave Principle: Key to Market Behavior by A.J. Frost and Robert R. Prechter, Jr., (c) Elliott Wave International, www.elliottwave.com

We have not covered these. You will not need to be concerned with these until the more advanced level. Since the labels D and E are only used in triangles they have been referenced as a note only. But when they are needed they must adhere to the correct degree notation as the 'A', 'B', and 'C' waves within their developing pattern.

Beginner Level: Practice Examination

The basics have been summarized for you and you are armed with quick references for these exams. The first exam is for practice and has 15 questions. It is a way to ensure you did not miss a few common points. If you struggled with the practice exam, you may want to consider a quick review of the Beginner chapters so you can ace your final exam that follows.

The answers will be found in the Exercise Appendix.

FIGURE 5.8   U.S. Industrial Production, Monthly

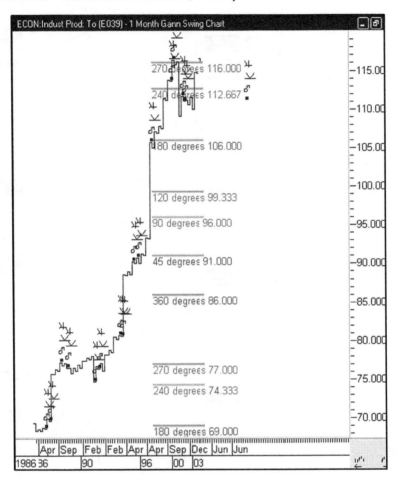

Source: Aerodynamic Investments Inc., © 1996–2012, Daily Market Report,
www.aeroinvest.com; Chart by Market Analyst 6, Copyright 1996–2012; data from CSI
Unfair Advantage, www.csidata.com.

Question 1: The chart in Figure 5.8 is a Gann swing chart of a monthly
Industrial Production fundamental data series. While price targets
and time targets are within the chart, these should not alter or change
your view about the Elliott Wave Principle. Draw a box around
swings that create an expanded flat in a corrective pull back.

Question 2: Put an X at the point in the rally you believe is the middle of
the strongest wave.

Question 3: Draw a box around wave iii of 3.

FIGURE 5.9   Bank Sector Stocks (BAC, WFC, MEL, ONE), Monthly

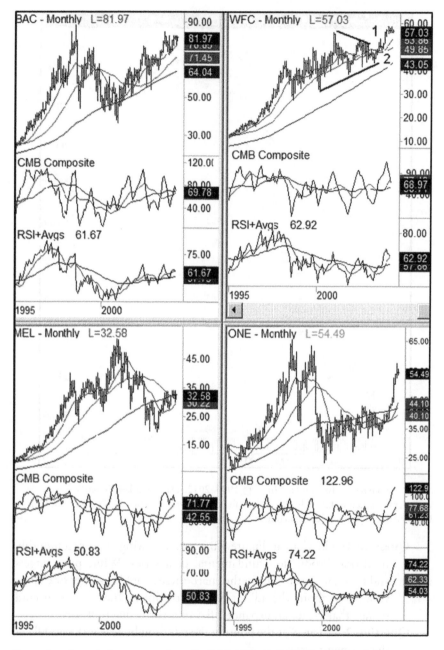

Source: Aerodynamic Investments Inc., © 1996–2012, Daily Market Report,
www.aeroinvest.com; TradeStation.

Figure 5.9 shows four banking sector stocks in a monthly time horizon. Wells Fargo (WFC) in the top right has developed a contracting triangle. None of the other stocks have created consolidations of the same pattern.

Question 4: Do you think WFC belongs to this sector or would it be better compared with stocks that form similar patterns at the same time?

Question 5: Is the rally for Wells Fargo (WFC) complete?

FIGURE 5.10 Crude Oil Futures, Weekly

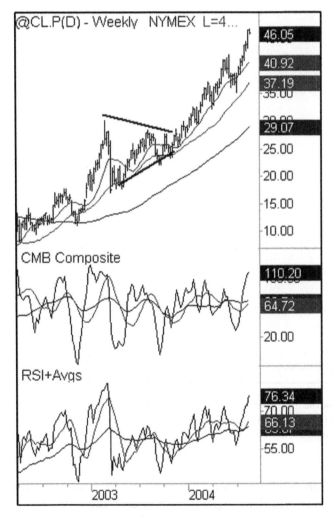

Source: Aerodynamic Investments Inc., © 1996–2012, Daily Market Report, www.aeroinvest.com; TradeStation.

Question 6: A weekly oil futures chart (Figure 5.10) is defining the thrust up from a contracting triangle. Draw a box to enclose an expanded flat correction from anywhere in this chart.

FIGURE 5.11   Copper Futures, Monthly

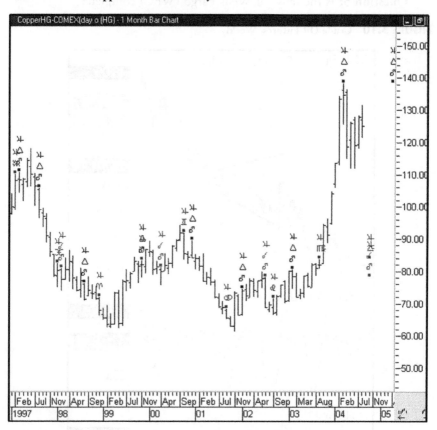

Source: Aerodynamic Investments Inc., © 1996–2012, Daily Market Report, www.aeroinvest.com; Chart by Market Analyst 6, (c) 1996–2012; data from CSI Unfair Advantage, www.csidata.com

Question 7: High Grade Copper futures in a monthly time horizon (Figure 5.11) have enjoyed a very strong rally that is not over. From the high a correction developed. Is the decline from the high a complete corrective pattern? Can you name the pattern?

FIGURE 5.12 Consumer Staples Index, Monthly

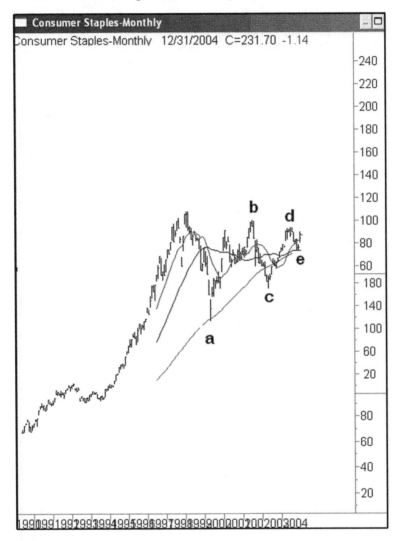

Source: Aerodynamic Investments Inc., © 1996–2012, Daily Market Report, www.aeroinvest.com; TradeStation; data from CSI Unfair Advantage, www.csidata.com.

Question 8: Figure 5.12 is a monthly chart of the S&P 500 Consumer Staples stock sector. A clear contracting triangle has just ended. Project a price target to show where the thrust out of this pattern will likely travel.

FIGURE 5.13   Oil/Gas Refining Index, Monthly

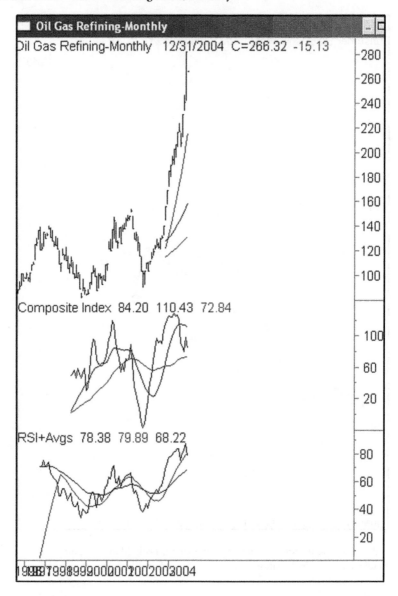

Source: Aerodynamic Investments Inc., www.aeroinvest.com; TradeStation; data from CSI
Unfair Advantage, www.csidata.com.

Question 9: Figure 5.13 shows the monthly data of the S&P 500 oil/gas refining stock sector. Label wave 1's resolution. Then mark wave '2'. Is wave '3' complete?

Question 10: Explain why the three wave swings that precede the strong third wave rally could *not* be viewed as a simple flat correction.

FIGURE 5.14   CAT, Weekly (left), Daily (right)

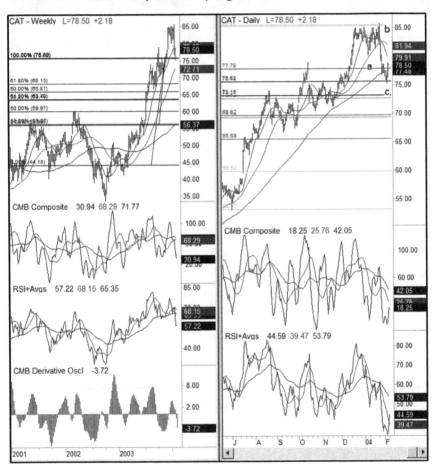

Source: Aerodynamic Investments Inc., © 1996–2012, Daily Market Report, www.aeroinvest.com; TradeStation.

Question 11: In the daily chart of Caterpillar (CAT) shown in Figure 5.14 the most recent data show an *expanded flat* pattern. Is it complete, and what must be present in wave 'c' to have a complete corrective pattern in place?

Question 12: In Figure 5.14 draw a box in the weekly chart to show an expanded flat correction.

FIGURE 5.15 Toronto Stock Exchange, Monthly

Question 13: Draw a box around an extending five-wave pattern in the monthly chart of the Toronto Stock Exchange Index.

Question 14: What is the name of the corrective pattern that begins the extending five-wave pattern?

Question 15: Draw a box to show the previous fourth wave range, which the decline from the high was targeting.

Beginner Level: Final Examination

The final exam consists of eight charts with questions. You may use any of the guide/summary sheets prepared for you in Chapter 5.

The answers will be found in the Exercise Appendix.

FIGURE 5.16   Final Exam 1

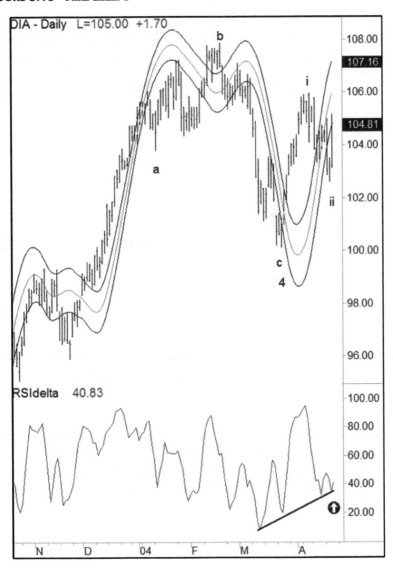

Source: Aerodynamic Investments Inc., Advanced Trading Seminar, TradeStation.

Question 1: Figure 5.16 is a daily chart of the DIA ETF for the Dow Jones Industrial Average. Pay no attention to the volatility bands running through the price data. You will have to become accustomed to reading wave structure through other analytics on your charts. Wave '4' has already been labeled for you. What kind of corrective pattern did the market develop?

FIGURE 5.17   Housing Sector Stocks (CTX Monthly, KBH Weekly, PHM Weekly)

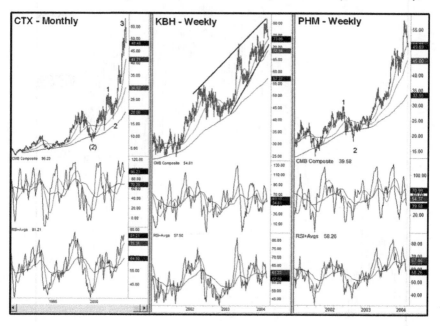

Source: Aerodynamic Investments Inc., © 1996–2012, Daily Market Report, www.aeroinvest.com; TradeStation.

Question 2: Figure 5.17 shows three housing stocks that enjoyed a spectacular emotional bubble that imploded in 2008. These charts were captured in 2004. KBH is forming a diagonal triangle termination pattern. CTX is clearly near the end of wave '3' up. Can a diagonal triangle end a third wave?

FIGURE 5.18   CVX, Monthly

Source: Aerodynamic Investments Inc., Seminars, TradeStation.

Question 3: The monthly chart for CVX in Figure 5.18 shows a complete five-wave pattern in the larger trend up. Wave 4 was a sizeable event. What kind of corrective pattern developed in the wave 'b of 4' position?

FIGURE 5.19   PDG, Daily

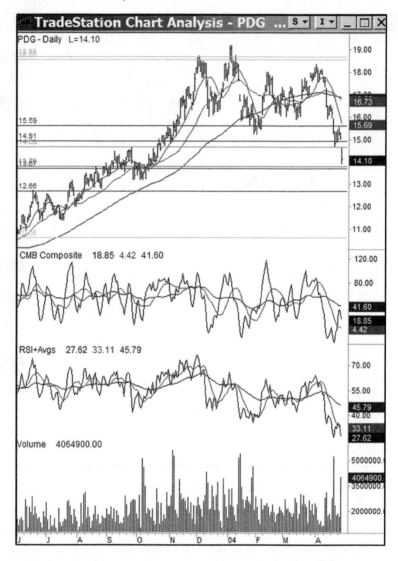

Source: Aerodynamic Investments Inc., © 1996–2012, Daily Market Report,
www.aeroinvest.com; TradeStation.

Question 4: Draw two boxes in the daily PDG chart (Figure 5.19) that
demonstrate zigzag corrective patterns. Draw two lines to show where
a diagonal triangle developed within the same chart.

FIGURE 5.20 OXY, Monthly

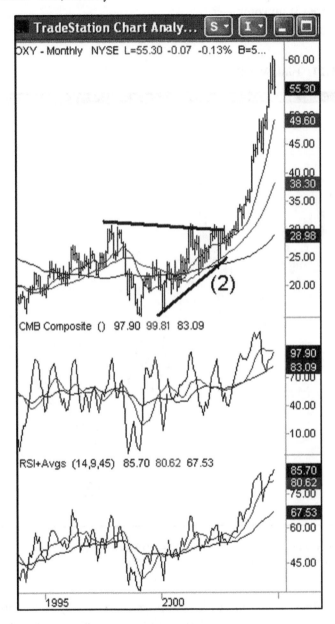

Source: Aerodynamic Investments Inc., Seminars, TradeStation.

Question 5: Figure 5.20 shows the monthly chart for OXY stock. Is wave (3) up complete?

FIGURE 5.21   Ford, Weekly

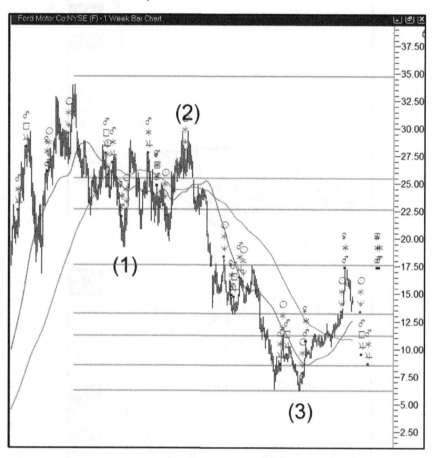

Source: Aerodynamic Investments Inc., © 1996–2012, Daily Market Report, www.aeroinvest.com; TradeStation.

Question 6: Ford (F) stock is displayed in a weekly time horizon in Figure 5.21. The wave interpretation in this chart suggests an impulse wave is unfolding that will create five waves down. Is wave (4) up complete now, and can the most recent pivot high near 17.50 be marked as (4)?

FIGURE 5.22 Nasdaq Index, Daily

Source: Aerodynamic Investments Inc., © 1996–2012, Daily Market Report, www.aeroinvest.com; TradeStation.

Question 7: The Nasdaq Index is shown in a daily chart in Figure 5.22. Identify where a contracting triangle developed.

FIGURE 5.23   Dow Jones Industrial Average, Point-and-Figure

Source: Aerodynamic Investments Inc., Seminars, TradeStation.

Question 8: Identify the location of two different contracting triangles in the point-and-figure chart for the Dow Jones Industrial Average in Figure 5.23.

The answers will be found in the Exercise Appendix.

■ ■ ■

When you are finished with the exams you will be ready to move on and further your skill level in *Advanced Elliott Wave Analysis: Complex Patterns, Intermarket Relationships, and Global Cash Flow Analysis*. I look forward to moving past the basics as the global chess board is a fascinating study when you apply the Elliott Wave Principle with skill. You will also learn ways to increase your probability for the wave interpretations you develop on your own. Do not think you are ready to do so at your current level, but you will have the skill to understand others' charts and recognize when the application of another's wave interpretation violates the basic tenants of the Wave Principle. That is an invaluable accomplishment. But we have so much more to cover together. We will surely meet again soon.

Exercise Appendix

Guidelines

Please do not read this Exercise Appendix until you have read the chapter referring you to this section in order to check your answers. It is nearly impossible for an author to control page design and the flow of text around charts in a chapter, so this will be a safer way to give you a chance to try a task on your own first. Each exercise is in the chapter it references, and you might want to make a copy of the chapter page before working on its task. That way you can start over if you need to. These exercises have helped others see where they had misunderstandings when they had thought the situation was crystal clear.

Introduction

Elliott Waves and Market Swings Are Not the Same

FIGURE I.1a INTC, Weekly

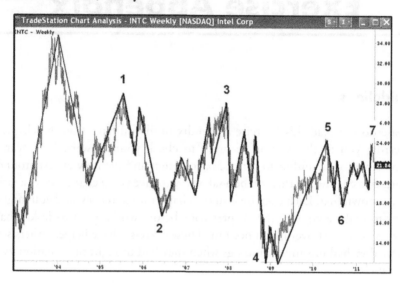

Source: Aerodynamic Investments Inc., © 1996–2012, Advanced Trading Seminar, www.aeroinvest.com; TradeStation.

FIGURE I.1b INTC, Weekly

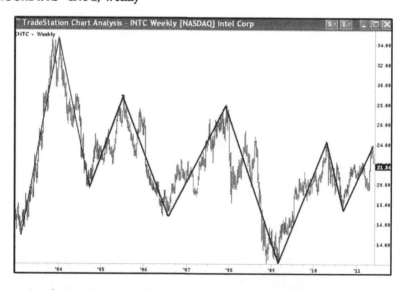

Source: Aerodynamic Investments Inc., © 1996–2012, Advanced Trading Seminar, www.aeroinvest.com; TradeStation.

Chapter 2
Impulse Waves Create Market Trends

FIGURE 2.3b Previous Fourth Wave of One Lesser Degree

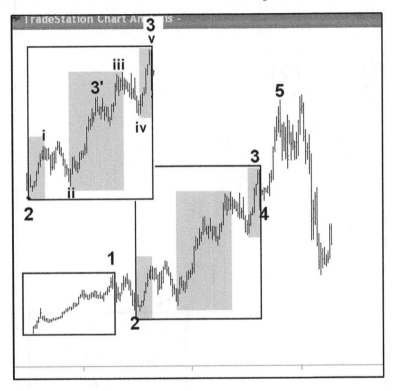

Source: Aerodynamic Investments Inc., © 1996–2012, Advanced Trading Seminar, www.aeroinvest.com; TradeStation.

FIGURE 2.5b Extending Five-Wave Patterns

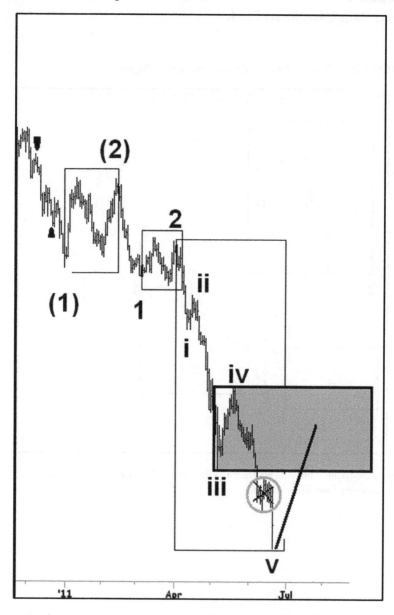

Source: Aerodynamic Investments Inc., © 1996–2012, Advanced Trading Seminar, www.aeroinvest.com; TradeStation.

FIGURE 2.8b Extending Five-Wave Pattern Exam

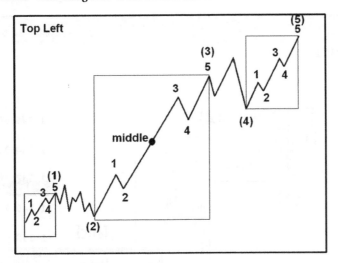

Source: Aerodynamic Investments Inc., © 1996–2012, Advanced Trading Seminar, www.aeroinvest.com; TradeStation.

FIGURE 2.10b S&P 500 Mini Futures, Intraday

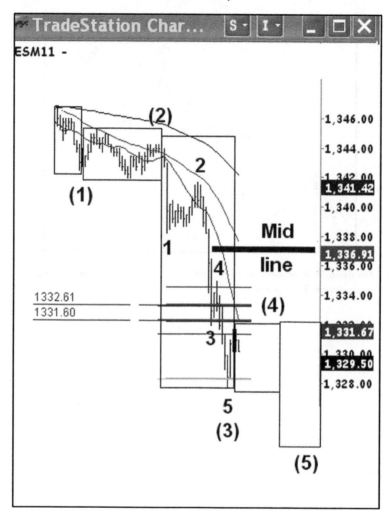

Source: Aerodynamic Investments Inc., © 1996–2012, Daily Market Report, www.aeroinvest.com; TradeStation.

Notice in Figure 2.10b that there is a correction with an N pattern. It does not retrace all the way back to the top of the rectangle. We call it a failure, because it does not return to the small rally into the top of the box the first time.

Waves 2 and 4 display the Guideline of Alternation. Wave 2 of (3) takes considerably more time to develop than did wave 4 of (3).

Now consider the amount of time in wave (2). You should know the small bounce up from wave 5 of (3) is only the start. It is too small to be all of wave (4). So I have drawn a box that would be proportional to wave (2). Wave (5) is missing entirely and needs to occur in this market move.

The market is the S&P 500 June 2011 mini futures contract in a seven-minute chart. Wave structure can be tracked in any time horizon.

IMPORTANT: *Do not* use tick data. Tick data are very short intraday displays where price bars are a fixed number of trades rather than trades that occurred within a fixed time interval. Using tick data destroys the wave pattern and you will not understand what hit you. Why? Patterns form, but they are very low probable scenarios because you have manipulated volume and sentiment into artificial packages.

Chapter 3

FIGURE 3.1b   A Zigzag Corrective Pattern

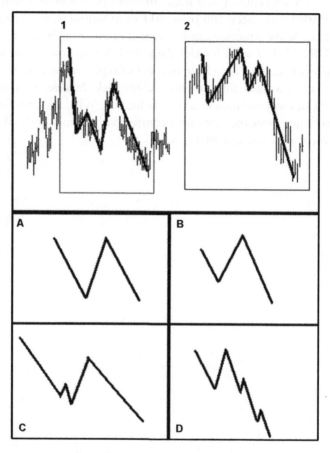

Source: Aerodynamic Investments Inc., © 1996–2012, Advanced Trading Seminar, www.aeroinvest.com; TradeStation.

FIGURE 3.2b A Corrective Zigzag Pattern Exercise

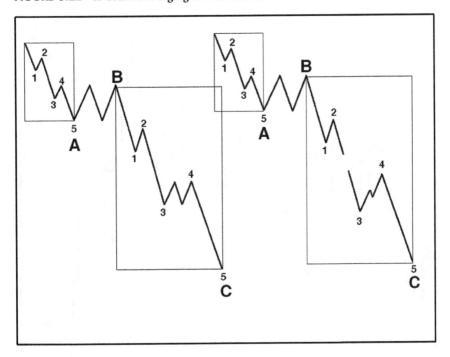

Source: Aerodynamic Investments Inc., © 1996–2012, Advanced Trading Seminar,
www.aeroinvest.com.

FIGURE 3.7b   USDJPY, Weekly

Source: Aerodynamic Investments Inc., © 1996–2012, Daily Market Report, www.aeroinvest.com.

Chapter 4
Diagonal Triangle Pattern

FIGURE 4.2a S&P 500 Cash Index, 120 Minutes

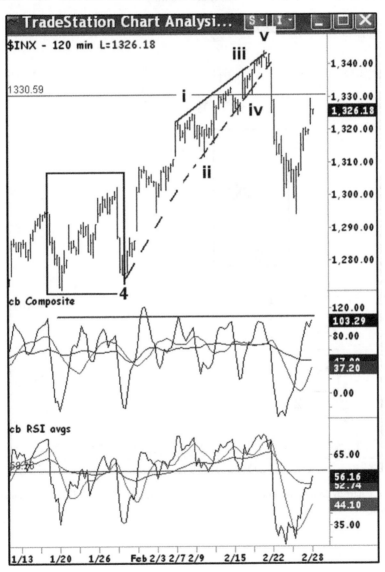

Source: Aerodynamic Investments Inc., © 1996–2012, Daily Market Report, www.aeroinvest.com; TradeStation.

Chapter 5
Beginner Level: Practice Examination

FIGURE 5.8a   U.S. Industrial Production, Monthly

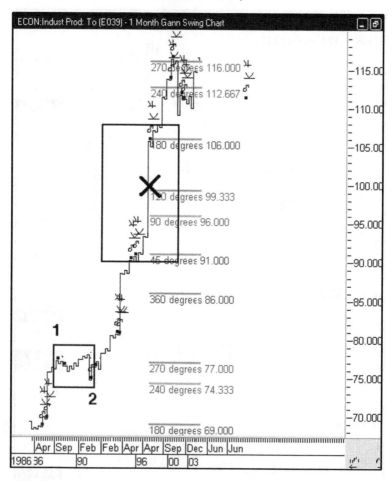

Source: Chart by Market Analyst 6, Copyright 1996–2012; data from CSI Unfair Advantage, www.csidata.com

Question 1: The chart in Figure 5.8 is a Gann swing chart of a monthly Industrial Production fundamental data series. While price targets and time targets are within the chart, these should not alter or change your view about the Elliott Wave Principle. Draw a box around swings that create an expanded flat in a corrective pullback.

ANSWER: While the footprint of the expanded flat is small in this chart, there is no mistaking the character of the corrective pattern. It cannot hide in different chart types or sizes—it has a look that rarely changes. One leg down, one leg up to a new high, one swing down that is sharp and breaks below the first leg down. The look and feel never changes. The rally into this correction has a clear five-wave pattern, which I have marked as wave 1.

Question 2: Put an X at the point in the rally you believe is the middle of the strongest wave.

ANSWER: By now, finding the strongest part of the move should be easy. Putting an X in the middle gives you the opportunity to make a price projection from the price low to the midline, and from the midline up to an equality swing. This rally is incomplete.

Question 3: Draw a box around wave iii of 3.

ANSWER: Wave 3 up is not complete, but finding wave iii of 3 is an easier question to answer. You just have to find the middle and work from that point to find five waves. Do this in all extending five-wave patterns.

FIGURE 5.9a Bank Sector Stocks (BAC, WFC, MEL, ONE) Monthly

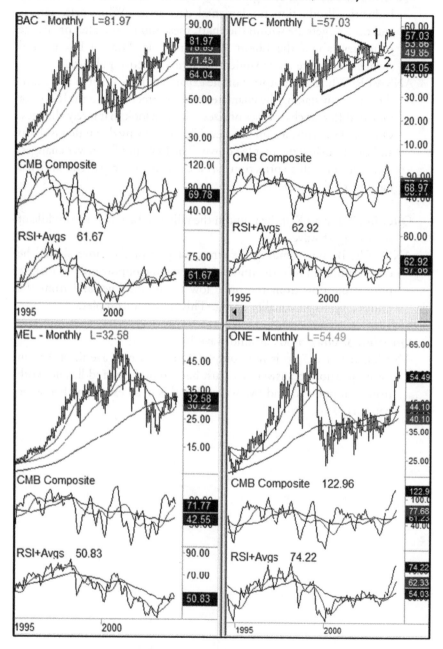

Source: Aerodynamic Investments Inc., © 1996–2012, Daily Market Report, www.aeroinvest.com; TradeStation.

Question 4: Do you think Wells Fargo (WFC) belongs to this sector or would it be better compared with stocks that form similar patterns at the same time?

ANSWER: Just because a different corrective pattern forms in a normally correlated stock sector does not mean something is wrong. But you surely want to know why three of the banks are breaking down so badly and Wells Fargo is trying to hold up on its own. This was the start of the mortgage crisis within the housing industry. The problems were in the charts long before the news was known publicly.

Question 5: Is the rally for Wells Fargo (WFC) complete?

ANSWER: The answer is no, if for no other reason than that I have labels 1 and 2 in the chart move just out of the triangle. It is too small for a thrust from such a large triangle, and there must be five waves to create a fifth wave.

FIGURE 5.10a   Crude Oil Futures, Weekly

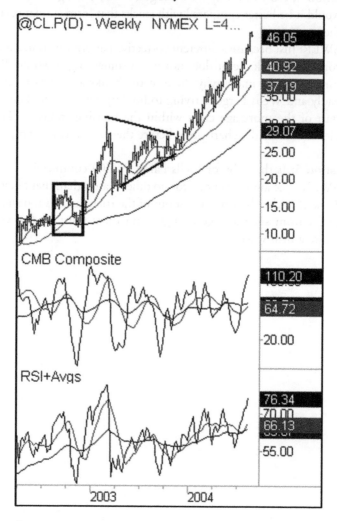

Source: Aerodynamic Investments Inc., © 1996–2012, Daily Market Report,
www.aeroinvest.com; TradeStation.

> **Question 6:** A weekly oil futures chart (Figure 5.10) is defining the
> thrust up from a contracting triangle. Draw a box to enclose an
> expanded flat correction from anywhere in this chart.
> ANSWER: What makes this question hard is that you are conditioned to
> the size of the contracting triangle. You were probably looking for
> something that looked as if it belonged in the same degree. But the

dead giveaway is the fact that a lone and clear five-wave decline is seen in a counter-trend move down. It cannot live by itself so the expanded flat pattern is revealed. This is a perfect demonstration of how you need to train your eye to see all sizes, but also you must remember that the look and feel never changes.

FIGURE 5.11a   Copper Futures, Monthly

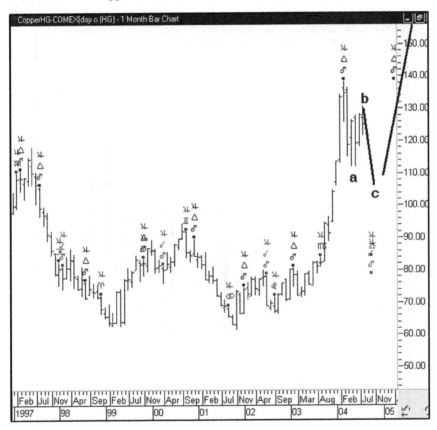

Source: Aerodynamic Investments Inc., © 1996–2012, Daily Market Report, www.aeroinvest.com; Chart by Market Analyst 6, Copyright 1996–2011; data from CSI Unfair Advantage, www.csidata.com.

Question 7: High Grade Copper futures in a monthly time horizon (Figure 5.11) have enjoyed a very strong rally that is not over. From the high a correction developed. Is the decline from the high a complete corrective pattern? Can you name the pattern?

ANSWER: If you got this one wrong, you need to run a lap around your office in penance! No correction can end with just a solitary five-wave counter-trend move. There is only one pattern that begins with five waves; it is the zigzag. You can be assured this question will appear again.

FIGURE 5.12a Consumer Staples Index, Monthly

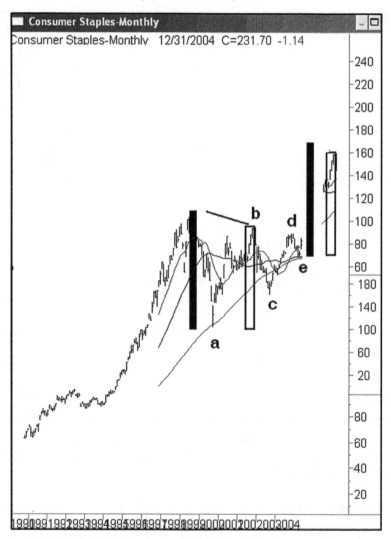

Source: Aerodynamic Investments Inc., © 1996–2012, www.aeroinvest.com; TradeStation; data from CSI Unfair Advantage, www.csidata.com.

Question 8: Figure 5.12 is a monthly chart of the S&P 500 Consumer Staples stock sector. A clear contracting triangle has just ended. Project a price target to show where the thrust out of this pattern will likely travel. ANSWER: There are two ways to make a measured move. One is slightly more conservative than the other. I show you both. The clear bar is a copy of the height from a to b instead of projecting b backwards.

FIGURE 5.13a Oil/Gas Refining Index, Monthly

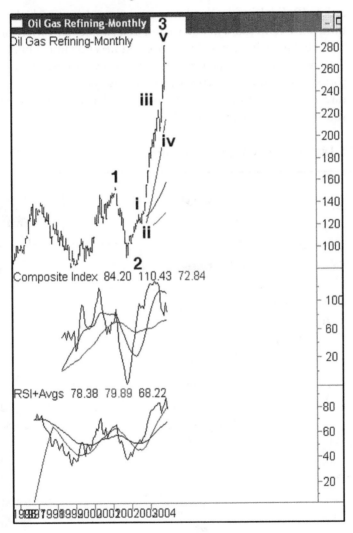

Source: Aerodynamic Investments Inc., © 1996–2012, www.aeroinvest.com; TradeStation; data from CSI Unfair Advantage, www.csidata.com.

Question 9: Figure 5.13 shows the monthly data of the S&P 500 Oil/ Gas Refining stock sector. Label wave 1's resolution. Then mark wave 2. Is wave 3 complete?

ANSWER: Wave 1 is just about as clear a five-wave pattern as you are going to be given. Wave '2' is a deep correction but does not break the origin of wave 1 that would violate the rule. Wave 3 is complete. Small hiccups of a pullback count as second and fourth waves.

Question 10: Explain why the three wave swings that precede the strong third wave rally could *not* be viewed as a simple flat correction.

ANSWER: The swing marked wave 1 could never be in the middle of a three-wave corrective pattern. It is clearly five waves. 'B' waves are corrections within corrections and will always be three-wave structures. So just because it has outer extremes that suggest a flat pattern, you should look at the internals.

FIGURE 5.14a   CAT, Weekly (left), Daily (right)

Question 11: In the daily chart of Caterpillar (CAT) shown in Figure 5.14 the most recent data show an *expanded flat* pattern. Is it complete, and what must be present in wave 'c' to have a complete corrective pattern in place?

ANSWER: All corrections that end with wave 'c' must develop five waves.

Question 12: In Figure 5.14, draw a box in the weekly chart to show an expanded flat correction.

ANSWER: The weekly chart of CAT has a larger expanded flat. If you wanted to find the same size as the one I conditioned your eye to see in the monthly, you likely had a tough time finding it. But it is a beauty!

FIGURE 5.15a Toronto Stock Exchange, Monthly

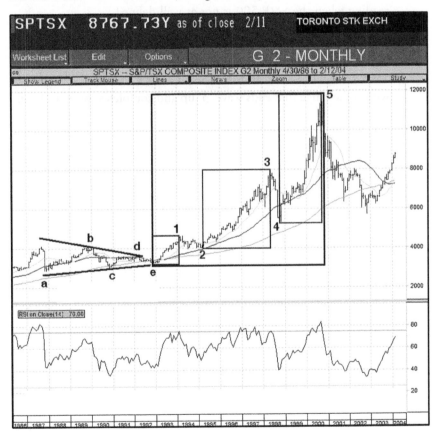

Source: Aerodynamic Investments Inc., © 1996–2012, www.aeroinvest.com; © Bloomberg LP. All rights reserved.

Question 13: Draw a box around an extending five-wave pattern in the monthly chart of the Toronto Stock Exchange Index shown in Figure 5.15.

ANSWER: I actually do not care if you put a box enclosing the entire five-wave pattern or just wave '3' of the pattern. As long as you found five waves and correctly read the internals, it will do for now.

Question 14: What is the name of the corrective pattern that begins the extending five-wave pattern?

ANSWER: A contracting triangle. This one took several years to complete all the swings, 'a' through 'e'. If you knew Toronto was defining a contracting triangle, the markets in the United States would have been much easier to determine and follow. Toronto often gives a clear reading when the S&P 500 is not as well defined.

Question 15: Draw a box to show the previous fourth wave range that the decline from the high was targeting.

ANSWER: I did not draw the box. The previous fourth wave is anywhere within the range that ends wave '3' up and completes wave '4' down.

Beginner Level: Final Examination

FIGURE 5.16 Final Exam 1

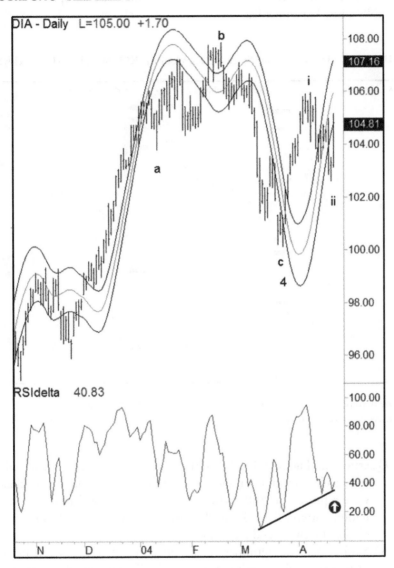

Source: Aerodynamic Investments Inc., Advanced Trading Seminar, TradeStation.

Question 1: Figure 5.16 is a daily chart of the DIA ETF for the Dow Jones Industrial Average. Wave '4' has already been labeled for you. What kind of corrective pattern did the market develop?
ANSWER: Expanded flat.

FIGURE 5.17 Housing Sector Stocks (CTX Monthly, KBH Weekly, PHM Weekly)

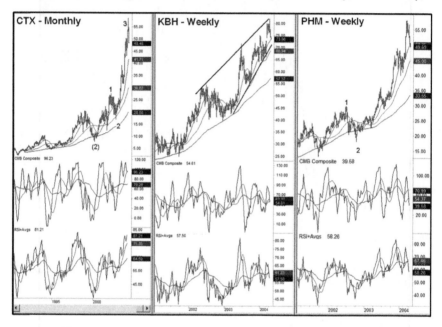

Source: Aerodynamic Investments Inc., © 1996–2012, Daily Market Report, www.aeroinvest.com, TradeStation.

Question 2: Figure 5.17 shows three housing stocks that enjoyed a spectacular emotional bubble that imploded in 2008. These charts were captured in 2004. KBH is forming a diagonal triangle termination pattern. CTX is clearly near the end of wave '3' up. Can a diagonal triangle end a third wave?
ANSWER: Yes, the termination diagonal triangle can develop in any fifth wave. In this case it is wave 'v of 3'. Termination does not mean it can only develop wave 'v of 5'.

FIGURE 5.18a   CVX, Monthly

Source: Aerodynamic Investments Inc., © 1996–2012, www.aeroinvest.com; TradeStation.

Question 3: The monthly chart for CVX in Figure 5.18 shows a complete five-wave pattern in the larger trend up. Wave 4 was a sizeable event. What kind of corrective pattern developed in the wave 'b' position?

ANSWER: You have to find wave 'b' in order to answer this question. It is a zigzag and is in Figure 5.18a. When wave 'b' is difficult to find work backwards. You know wave 'c of 4' must develop a five-wave pattern. Where wave 'c' begins is also where the 'b' wave ended. Suddenly the pattern reveals itself.

FIGURE 5.19a   PDG, Weekly

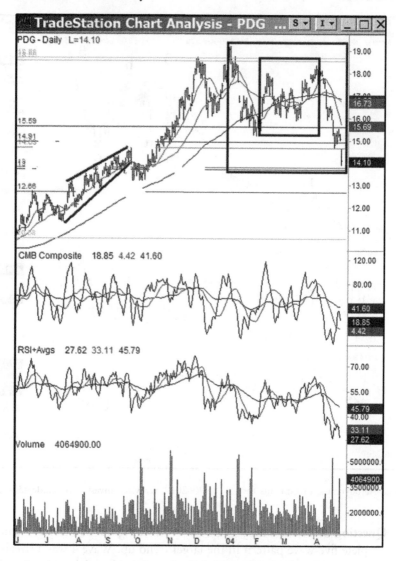

Source: Aerodynamic Investments Inc., © 1996–2012, Daily Market Report,
www.aeroinvest.com; TradeStation.

Question 4: Draw two boxes in the daily PDG chart that demonstrate zigzag corrective patterns. Draw two lines to show where a diagonal triangle developed within the same chart.

ANSWER: The zigzags are contained one within the other. Wave 'B' within the correction is also a zigzag.

The termination diagonal triangle might be difficult to see because the market does not fall back to the origin. It is exceptionally rare to see this, but it is explained by the parabolic move that follows. The small correction that follows immediately after the wedge does fall back to a previous fourth wave, however.

FIGURE 5.20 OXY, Monthly

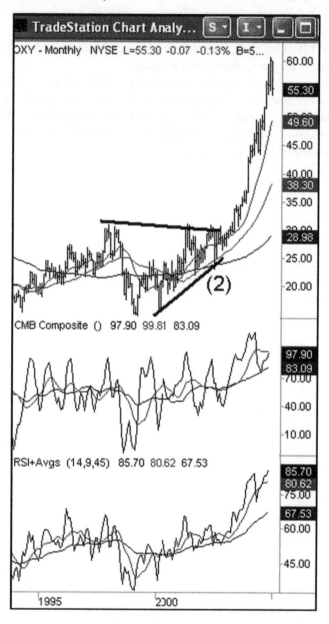

Source: Aerodynamic Investments Inc., Seminars, TradeStation.

Question 5: Figure 5.20 shows the monthly chart for OXY stock. Is wave (3) up complete?

ANSWER: No. You cannot have a triangle that stands by itself in a second wave position. Wave (3) up is incomplete because the implied start is incorrect.

FIGURE 5.21 Ford, Weekly

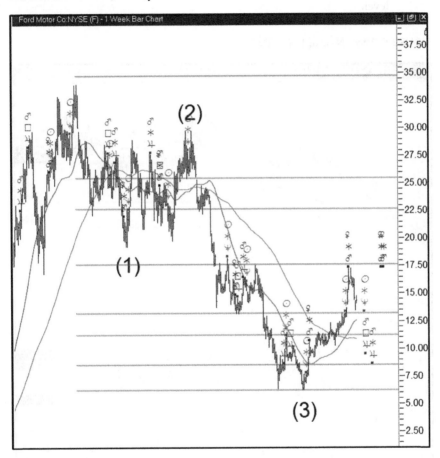

Source: Aerodynamic Investments Inc., © 1996–2012, Daily Market Report, www.aeroinvest.com; TradeStation.

Question 6: Ford (F) stock is displayed in a weekly time horizon in Figure 5.21. The wave interpretation in this chart suggests an impulse wave is unfolding that will create five waves down. Is wave (4) up complete now, so that the most recent pivot high near 17.50 can be marked as (4)?

ANSWER: It is a complete zigzag correction. Done. However, you have to ask if this is only wave A of (4). We have to address that in the next level.

FIGURE 5.22a   Nasdaq Index, Daily

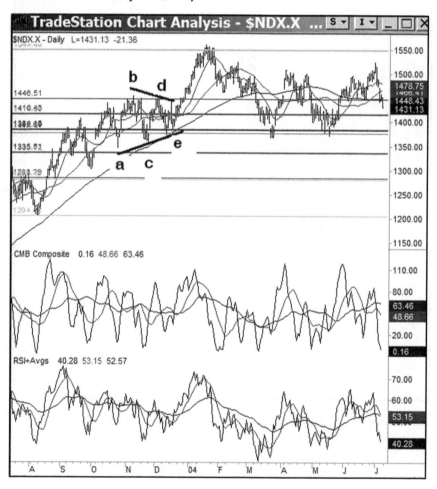

Source: Aerodynamic Investments Inc., © 1996–2012, Daily Market Report, www.aeroinvest.com; TradeStation.

Question 7: The Nasdaq Index is shown in a daily chart in Figure 5.22. Identify where a contracting triangle developed.

FIGURE 5.23a Dow Jones Industrial Average, Point-and-Figure

Source: Aerodynamic Investments Inc., Seminars, TradeStation.

Question 8: Identify the location of two different contracting triangles in the point-and-figure chart for the Dow Jones Industrial Average shown in Figure 5.23.

ANSWER: You are correct as long as you did not pick the second wave. There are three possible locations, since we cannot see more than a shape. That is all that is needed in point-and-figure charts.

About the Author

Constance M. Brown, CMT, is the founder of Aerodynamic Investments, Inc. Connie has been a professional trader with extensive global experience trading futures markets since 1991. Her hedge fund was closed in 2003 after an annual return of 68 percent. She continues to trade, consult institutional traders, and teach from South Carolina.

The Market Technicians Association in New York selected her book, *Technical Analysis for the Trading Professional,* as required study for the final certification examination for the CMT (Chartered Market Technician; visit www.mta.org).

She has written eight books and was the recent editor of the *Journal of Technical Analysis.* The Market Technicians Association distributes the *Journal* to more than 70 countries.

About Aerodynamic Investments, Inc.

Please visit the web site of Aerodynamic Investments Inc. at www.aeroinvest .com to review a current list of services for:

- Investments
- Current Market Analysis
- Education Seminars

E-mail communications can be sent to: support@aeroinvest.com.

Index

Printed and bound by CPI Group (UK) Ltd, Croydon, CR0 4YY

16/04/2025

14658449-0005